Fearless
Conversations
with a
Limitless God

Fearless Conversations
with a Limitless God

VEIRDRE JACKSON, EdD

Printed in the United States of America

Cover and interior design by Faith Hague

Art by Zintelligence Design

Photo on page 159 and on back cover by Ashley Craig—A Digital Design

The image on page 12 is printed with permission of Steps of Growth
©2019 Diane Wagenhals and Lakeside Global Institute.

Library of Congress Control Number 2019904317

ISBN 978-0-9844804-9-4

2 4 6 8 10 9 7 5 3 1 paperback

Dedication

THE PHRASE IRON SHARPENS IRON is a term from Proverbs 27:17 (NIV) *"As iron sharpens iron, so one person sharpens another."* It represents the refining process of one blade being used to rub against another to sharpen the edges to make it more efficient in its use. The women I have asked to be a part of the stories, messages, and conversations in this book represent that sharpening process in my life. At key moments of not being sure that I had what it took to continue to be effective in what God wanted to use me for, they sharpened my walk and accountability. The rubbing process sometimes created sparks, often brought us closer, and has always left me more polished in the end. I am so grateful for their vulnerability, their authenticity, and their stories, which have made me better in my journey. I dedicate this book to those women who have blessed my soul and have loved me through the hardest times in my life but never let me stay dull because as iron sharpens iron it underscores that our sorrows, our stories, and our successes are connected, and God has called us to fellowship, love, and accountability. Thank you, ladies, for just being who God has called you to be. I dedicate this book to you.

Jael Lin Jackson
Malinda Fife
Jessie Seneca
Tina Pelzer
Cheryl Hurley
Esther Moore
Ashley Craig
Obioma Martin
Dale Sharpe Lee
Gina Hackett Curry
Deb Studevan
Chanel Mulbah
Celeste Taylor
Sonya Deloatch

Contents

Foreword by Diane Wagenhals. 9

Introduction to the Steps of Growth 11

F.E.A.R. Is a Perspective 15

Core Beliefs Shape Your Battle Plan 30

Stepping Out of the Hiding Places of Shame. 48

Fix Your Focus on Faith 67

Stepping into Peace. 82

Power and Purpose Are a Passion, Not a Platform. . 97

You Are Enough. 112

The Revelation of Gratitude 129

Joy with My Soul 143

Resources 157

Acknowledgments 158

About the Author 159

Foreword

BECOMING A CHRISTIAN and being a Christian are two different aspects of our journey in life. There is the moment when we realize there is a God who loves us and extends His love personally to us through His Son, Jesus Christ. When we embrace the invitation to accept Christ as our Lord and Savior, we become a Christian. Most of us feel enormous gratitude, relief, and purpose in this moment.

Then there is the actual journey of being a Christian, a journey of learning and growing, seeking ways to better understand what God wants for each of us. The journey involves finding ways to be the hands and feet of Jesus, to put our faith into action as we learn to love God with all our strength, heart, soul, and mind and to love our neighbors as ourselves.

A few decades ago when I was first writing curriculum for leadership training in parenting education, it occurred to me that the stage has to be intentionally set to walk through a process to where one can confidently and competently put information, concepts, approaches, principles, and skills into action. In playing with this idea, I came up with the image of a stairway to growth and change. This became my Steps of Growth.

I was thrilled when Veirdre called me to tell me about her soon-to-be-published book. I was humbled as she explained how she had used the Steps of Growth as the platform on which she could help her readers appreciate each journey of becoming transformed as a Christian woman. I was honored when she asked me to write this foreword.

Veirdre and I met over a decade ago when we both attended an event where Dr. Sandra Bloom spoke. Through God's divine providence, we were seated next to each other and soon became engaged in a deep and meaningful conversation. We commented on feeling as if we had been brought together by God to share the experience of the event together and that we would build an important relationship.

Veirdre and I stayed connected, and she began attending the courses I had authored for the Institute for Family Professionals (now Lakeside Global Institute). Lakeside Global Institute is a program of Lakeside Educational Network providing professional development in the United States. Veirdre and I worked together at several conferences, sharing a passion for helping parents, caregivers, and professionals who work in early childhood settings to better understand the needs of young children. Veirdre became a trainer for Lakeside Global Institute and in recent years has taught trauma courses we provide in collaboration with Jefferson University.

Veirdre is an amazing person who has dedicated her life to serving God and empowering women. As she invites you to become aware of your journey up the Steps of Growth, know you are being guided by a person who can provide you with specific ways to love the Lord your God with all your strength, heart, soul, and mind. You can also expect to learn ways to love others as well as yourself. By taking this journey one step at a time, you can celebrate each new awareness, deepen your understanding, take action, and finally reflect on your experience. You will more clearly see how God works through you, just as He has been working through Veirdre as she authored this book. I wish for you new insight and renewed passion for your journey in life as you engage in the book's content, recommended activities, and discussions. May it bring you even closer to God and clearer about your journey in life as you learn and grow through her gentle guidance.

—*Diane Wagenhals, Director of Lakeside Global Institute*

Introduction to the Steps of Growth

SO OFTEN IN THE PROCESS of creating change, a mistake is made. For example, after a conference, a Bible study meeting, or a women's event, someone states, "Well, you heard what you need to do, so now you should be doing it!"

Women leave these experiences excited but then become disappointed or frustrated with themselves because they heard what to do but aren't seeing the change in their everyday lives. In reality, just knowing information only moves a person out of the basement to a place of awareness. There is an entire step to the process that is often missed, and that step is gaining understanding of broken patterns, repeated mistakes, or misguided mindsets, to make informed change that leads to creating intentional, effective action.

In *Fearless Conversations with a Limitless God*, I am providing you with practical steps to examine where you are—even if it is in the basement. I invite you to become aware of what is in your way, gain understanding of your life patterns, and engage in a change process, to create a plan for action, and be able to reflect on new practices and experience wisdom of lessons learned.

In each of the chapters of this book, it is my passion to deepen your understanding of the spoken Word of God by connecting Biblical principles to simple object lessons, practical instruction, and the intimate character of our relational God through conversations He has with characters sprinkled through the pages of Scripture. We serve a loving, faithful, powerful God who has made freedom available to each of us, and it starts with making the mental choice to choose life and choose it abundantly. However, that is usually not a quick fix but a journey—and sometimes a battle. Years of broken patterns, emotional hurt, and a distorted thought life can leave us not really living, but simply surviving.

Fearless Conversations Steps of Growth

Fearless Conversations with a Limitless God meets women in their "hiding places" where they are often wanting and wishing for more but don't have the practical steps and tools to move forward. The unique design of this daily devotional combines practical lessons from neuroscience, the power of conversation, and intentional tools from Biblical instructions. In each chapter, you will use the Steps of Growth framework, which walks women physically, emotionally, mentally, and spiritually out of a "basement" mindset into a place of reflection and freedom. Each chapter reveals a moment in time where Christ met different individuals at specific points in their lives and interrupted their broken belief systems, misguided self-narratives, and tragic stories of shame and regret and exposed their "hiding places" to free them to walk in a fearless confidence, accessing promises meant to be kept and used as a weapon to unravel the lies of the enemy.

Many of life's battles are won or lost in the mind. With every test, we stand at the crossroads of being bitter or better, broken or built up, victim or victor. This book is for every woman who is ready to break the cycle of toxic thoughts that contradict God's promises of life and abundance. Renewing your mind is not just a childhood memory verse to be tucked away for safe keeping, but it's also a divine command for daily victorious living. *Fearless Conversations with a*

Limitless God brings to life Biblical principles that confirm practical science found in how the brain responds to stress, toxic cycles, and broken mental patterns. It does this with intentional daily habits that shift your perspective, strengthen your faith, and give purpose to your story through Biblical instruction, trauma-informed approaches, and self-discovery.

I am so excited to go on this journey with you as we take intentional steps forward. Take your time and be patient with the process. The book is designed for you to take one step per day and meditate on what God is revealing to you. Certain steps will be more emotional than others, so be gentle with yourself. In each chapter, when you arrive at the step of understanding, I have embedded the opportunity to listen in on "Iron Sharpens Iron" conversations with women who have had a deep impact on my own journey through life. Based on life experiences, revelations of God's impact on their lives, and practical understanding of what women are struggling with, each conversation creates small, intimate moments of real "girl talk." These conversations unpack dialogue and rich understanding on important topics that affect our daily lives as women, including the impact of shame, peace, power, fear, faith, being enough, gratitude, and more—with the cameras rolling!

Each chapter also uses the power of being still, meditating on God's grace, and using the therapeutic approach of adult coloring to carve out calm, focused moments that rewire the brain. At the end of each chapter, a Fearless Conversations theme is artistically captured and provided to give you time to connect worship, prayer, music, and stillness while you focus on the creative act of coloring. Coloring has been found to reduce anxiety, increase focus, build awareness, and provide clarity. When you take the time to calm your mind, your brain enters a relaxed state by focusing on the present and blocking out the nonstop thinking we all experience. As a result, you reach a place of calm that relieves your brain from the daily stresses of life and allows you to continue to refresh and restore.

The entire experience of *Fearless Conversations with a Limitless God* is designed to provide you with Biblical principles for each topic and also to create an opportunity for you to think deeply about an intentional process for moving into your place of healing. It's a healing that will leave you feeling brave enough to take on all that God provides, and also fearless in taking back anything the enemy has tried to steal from you in the process.

Throughout this book, I have quoted Scripture from a number of different versions of the Bible because some translations better illuminated a specific point I was trying to make. The abbreviations for these are as follows:

AMP = Amplified Bible

CEB = Common English Bible

ESV = English Standard Version

MSG = The Message

NIV = New International Version

NKJV = New King James Version

NLT = New Living Translation

Fearless Conversations with a Limitless God

F.E.A.R.
Is a Perspective

Coming Out of the Basement: Wired for F.E.A.R.

If an impala can leap 10 feet high and 30 feet wide, how is it contained behind 3-foot-tall zoo barricades? This is the question Paul Jolicoeur asks in his article *The Barrier between You and Your Dreams.* And the answer is profound: An impala will leap only if it can visualize where it will land. Yes, this amazing creature with innate ability and power creates "self-imposed limitations." It's confined by limits created in its own mind because of the fear of the unknown.

Wow, how many of us can say that the impala is not the only God-created creature that does that? Like the impala, many of us are confined by walls of fear, doubt, insecurity, and self-preservation.

Those were probably many of the same emotions the Israelites struggled with as they ran with disbelief from their enslaved homes in Egypt toward the possibility of freedom in the promised land. Already unsure of the future, conflicted between possibility and frantic escape, they get to the Red Sea.

EXODUS 14:10–12 (NKJV) *And when Pharaoh drew near, the children of Israel lifted their eyes, and behold, the Egyptians marched after them. So they were very afraid, and the children of Israel cried out to the Lord. Then they said to Moses, "Because there were no graves in Egypt, have you taken us away to die in the wilderness? Why have you so dealt with us, to bring us up out of Egypt? Is this not the word that we told you in Egypt, saying, 'Let us alone that we may serve the Egyptians'? For it would have been better for us to serve the Egyptians than that we should die in the wilderness."*

Do you see what happened there? As fear rose up and a very real sense of feeling trapped took over, the thought of possibility evaporated. That's just how fear grips our heart, mind, and rational thought. The Israelites actually shifted their mindset from victorious escapee, running to freedom, to victim of an attack with certain death. Instead of focusing their attention on moving forward and believing in a God who had already shown his ability for escape through the 10 plagues that got them to this point, they shifted their attention back to the broken place of enslavement and allowed their emotions to take over the race.

Fear is an interesting emotion. It protects us from dangerous situations and can help us to not make dumb decisions, but it also can keep us from taking necessary risks that are vital to doing what we know is necessary and a part of our steps forward. When used properly, fear can be lifesaving as a natural stress response signal to take action. We are wired to survive, and our fight, flight, and freeze brain responses send a flood of chemical responses to our defense, including cortisol and adrenaline, which are meant to happen momentarily and sporadically for protective measures. If this release becomes engrained and recycled over time, however, it becomes a life-damaging reaction that keeps people sick, stuck, confused, and preferring the familiar place of enslavement over the uncertainty of freedom. It shifts from a temporary signal to an entrenched lifestyle. Our brain is "use dependent," so repeated use of toxic stress and fear can become the trained normal to our mindset instead of the refreshing mental renewal God offers each of us, and that cycle comes at a cost.

We can think of fear as an acronym, F.E.A.R. How we view that acronym will determine how we respond when fear shows up. In the Enhancing Trauma Awareness course at Lakeside Global Institute, students are taught to examine the lenses through which they look at life. Some of us will look at F.E.A.R. through a dark lens on life and see very few possibilities when this emotion enters our experiences. In those cases, we perceive F.E.A.R. to mean Forget Everything And Run. Through this dark lens, fear may provide a temporary relief of escape, but it never allows us to solve any problems.

Other people may look at F.E.A.R. through dotted glasses. These lenses on life are dotted with the residue of life's past experiences, and they cause people to have a hindered or obstructed view of life. They can't seem to see past those obstructions, and in moments that open the door for F.E.A.R. to show up on the scene, they look at F.E.A.R. and life as Finding Excuses And Reasons. Now don't get me wrong, those obstructions, blocked spots, and hindered smudges that cover their perspective on life may have been traumatic, and their view is rightly limited, but this perspective will do little to move the person out of the cycle of learned helplessness and into the promised place of abundance on the other side of excuses and reasons.

Some others may have a greater ability to see life more fully, but their lenses of F.E.A.R. have scratches from past hurt and disappointment that have never healed and have begun to diminish their expectations for anything other than a poor fate. Although they may try to polish their lenses with new risks and steps of progress, the abrasiveness of past mistakes, failures, and mishaps has this person view F.E.A.R. as Failure Expected And Received. When this mindset controls our focus, what we expect is what we receive.

After one of my presentations on fear, a participant enlightened me to another lens, which can be described as the rose-colored glasses. She shared her pattern of not wanting to see or deal with the truth, and her perspective of F.E.A.R. was Fake Everything And Repeat. It was easier for her to keep her mask on and not reckon with the truth of the brokenness in her life. It may have been easier on her comfort level with life, but it was a barrier to really living.

Each one of these distorted views of the tool of fear actually helps us understand that fear is not just in our head. It actually lives in our body. When fear shifts from lifesaving as a temporary signal to life-damaging as a cycle or way of being, it changes far more than external situations and circumstances. When we become aware of this truth and the shackle on our mind it creates, we can begin to understand why our God would give the command to "fear not" more than 80 times throughout Scripture, more often than any other command—lifesaving instruction.

Building Your Awareness: Polish Your Lenses

EXODUS 14:10–14 (MSG) *As Pharaoh approached, the Israelites looked up and saw them—Egyptians! Coming at them! They were totally afraid. They cried out in terror to God. They told Moses, "Weren't the cemeteries large enough in Egypt so that you had to take us out here in the wilderness to die? What have you done to us, taking us out of Egypt? Back in Egypt didn't we tell you this would happen? Didn't we tell you, 'Leave us alone here in Egypt—we're better off as slaves in Egypt than as corpses in the wilderness.'" Moses spoke to the people: "Don't be afraid. Stand firm and watch God do his work of salvation for you today. Take a good look at the Egyptians today for you're never going to see them again. God will fight the battle for you. And you? You keep your mouths shut!"*

God gives us the command "fear not" for our physical, mental, and spiritual well-being. Not only will fear inhibit our ability to think critically and impair wise decision-making, as seen by the Israelites in verses 10 to 12, but it also robs us of sleep, changes our immune systems, is associated with seven out of 10 major diseases traced back to toxic thinking, and changes the architecture of the brain. In our passage, after a conversation with God, Moses's instruction breaks the momentum of the cycle of fear pulsing through the Israelites' minds and bodies. God knew that for more than 400 years, fear had been the life cycle of the enslaved Israelites, and in a declarative moment, He puts an end to this triggered response by taking them to the brink of an inescapable place and commanding them to fear not, stand firm, and watch. In this moment, He is going to remove the darkness, hindrances, and scratched lenses of every Israelite standing on the shore. He will remove the dysfunctional lenses they had been using to make their way through their lives and replace them with polished, magnified lenses that will allow them to see a new normal—one with God's hand showing up in a way that is miraculous, unquestionable, and profound. He didn't want them to miss it by scrambling for weapons or running for cover or being confused by the adrenaline coursing through their bodies. No, fear not, stand firm, and watch!

When was the last time you did something really scary—the kind of scary that knots your stomach and has your heart racing and your knees knocking. The kind of scary that has you feeling like you have lost all control. Yeah, I had one of those moments in my life. Because of past mistakes and failings, I spent most of my days walking around with the scratched lenses mentioned in section 1. In my mind, I constantly questioned my self-worth, competence, and capacity. Coming out of years of a toxic work environment, hiding behind workaholic behavior to find my value, I struggled to see, hear, or feel God. But I had a plan for my future: My eye was on an executive position. Yes, that would make me finally feel whole, achieved, and enough. When the enemy sets a trap, he sets it well. That "ideal" position was placed in my lap. I quit my current job, ready to start new beginnings with *my plan*. And before I could even start the job, it disappeared. I had nothing to go back to and nothing to go forward to. Stuck—no money, no job, poor health from a decade of toxic stress, and a distorted view of my value and my relationship with God. In the middle of my *Red Sea* moment, I felt trapped and horribly afraid, ashamed, and unworthy, and the *"I told you so ..."* began from my scratched lens on life. And in the middle of it all, during a rant with God blaming Him for not going along with *my plan,* He sat me down through illness and created a window of clarity for me to break the cycle. In the quiet from my sick bed, He began to open up my spirit and pour out the vision He had planned for me all along. Not able to do anything except stay in bed, I wrote for 10 days while He filled my spirit with *His Plan*. On the 11th day, the legal documents for my own business arrived at my door, and He told me to move forward. Fear not. Stand still. Watch. For three years now, I have watched Him do more with this fragile life than I could have ever imagined. With a change in perspective, you can have a new perspective on F.E.A.R.

"Change the way you see things, and the things you see will change." —Dr. Wayne Dyer

Shifting how we view things and what we choose to focus on shifts our direction, our purpose, and our perspective on ourselves, our lives, and our God.

For Everything A Reason

Face Everything And Rise

Faith Erases All Reservations

New Language

Take a moment and reflect on how you have been thinking about the role of fear in your life. If it is anything except a response signal to act and move toward more life saturated in abundance, polish your lenses and reframe your perspective. Create a new acronym for fear next:

F _orgivenes_

E _____

A _____

R _____

The Conversation for Understanding Patterns of Fear

Why does God spend so much time challenging us to not fear and to manage our thoughts by renewing our minds? (Romans 12:2)

When toxic fear shows up, it often brings a few cousins for the ride.

Threat. Anxiety. Worry. Panic. Terror.

When emotions like these show up, how do you respond? Which lens do you usually reach for first? And how does that lens help you or hinder you in that moment?

I panic inside -- my heart races --
I'm frozen thinking the worst will
happen, I'm to blame I'm
going to loose everything. The lens
Hinder me for hours!

Whichever behavior we spend the most time speaking to (even to ourselves) repeats itself. That repeated behavior becomes our traits, and our traits become our brain state. If you think of your brain as a seed, wherever that seed is planted, it will pull from the soil to grow roots. Based on the environment, patterns, and experiences the brain is buried in, healthy or toxic, it will take root and grow. As the brain matures, the mind begins to develop coping strategies to survive the environment it has been planted in. We are designed to be survival creatures, so whether the soil that surrounds our mind is healthy or toxic, the brain will adapt to survive the experience. That adaptation brings on healthy or maladaptive coping strategies. Healthy or not, these responses to the environment that our mind is placed in become rooted and become our normal. Healthy or not, they help us survive.

But the tricky part to this root system in our mind is that it *must take care of myself...*

breaks through the surface of our life and produces our core belief system. Our patterned response for survival will shape what we believe to be true about the world around us, the people near us, and the God in us. Our God spends so much time challenging us to not fear and take captive our thoughts (2 Corinthians 10:5) because He knows how we are wired and how a distorted root system within our mind will distort our beliefs about everything around us and anything He brings to us. And when our belief system is distorted, toxic, and malnourished, the only fruit that can be served to others as outward behaviors from a toxic source is rotten or withered.

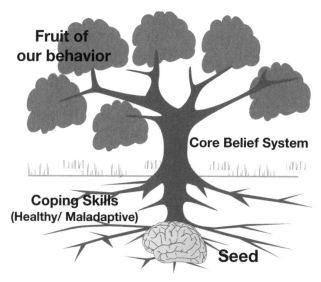

Fruit of our behavior

Core Belief System

Coping Skills
(Healthy/ Maladaptive)

Seed

Unlike authors of self-help books or "how-to" tips, I share this analogy to shift your focus from trying to pick off and throw away the withered fruit. Because we know that we could pick withered fruit all day, but if we don't address the root, the withered fruit will just return.

Thinking about how you respond when fear (and his cousins) show up is an opportunity to become critical and intentional about what you believe about the power of that fear. Understand how that *go-to response* has served you in the past, helping you to survive, but now be intentional and transparent about asking if it actually serves you well *today*. Write the coping strategies you use when fear enters the room. Take your time. Be still. Be honest. Ask God to reveal to you what you have been depending on to survive.

Examples: smoking, drinking, walks, breathing, shopping excessively, overeating, avoiding, cursing, fighting, exercise, running, isolating, praying, etc.

Healthy and Maladaptive Strategies to Cope

Walks (H)   Doing for others (m;H)

Drinking Wine (m)

Shopping (m)

Worship Music (H)

Reflect on **2 Timothy 1:7 (NKJV)** *For God has not given us a spirit of fear, but of **power and of love and of a sound mind**.* Now cross anything from the list that does not reflect the power, love, and sound mind God has promised you. Think about life-giving coping strategies that promote your inheritance of Power. Love. Sound Mind. (For examples of Fearless Coping Skills, go to our website, https://livingstrongllc.com/fearlessly-free-downloads/, for a free download to carry with you to create a shift in your root system.)

Go here!

_____

_____

_____

Next begin to become honest about what is in your soil, your environment, that is no longer healthy for you. It's time to till the soil that is feeding your mind. For me, I had to change jobs and step out as an entrepreneur. What is God revealing that needs to be removed from your soil? Identify people, experiences, self-talk, and spaces and places that are toxic and have fueled the distorted view of the truth of what God says you deserve, you were made for, and you are entitled to. **Jeremiah 29:11 (NIV)** *"For I know the plans I have for you," declares the Lord, "plans to prosper you and not to harm you, plans to give you hope and a future."*

Video

Go to the Fearless Conversations with a Limitless God Video Companion at https://gumroad.com/livingstrongllc#. Enter the

discount code m88hm52 to get access to the video content for free. (As you work through each chapter in this book, there will be an accompanying "Iron Sharpens Iron" Fearless Conversations video for you to watch to gain greater insights from other women on their own Fearless journeys.) As you listen as these women share their personal stories of pain, victory, and revelation, answer the following questions. What is God revealing to you about conquering any unhealthy perspective of fear?

How does fear change our brain and keep us in the basement?

_____

_____

_____

_____

How does fear show up as pride?

_____

_____

_____

_____

How can changing a fearful mindset shift us to purposeful living?

_____

_____

_____

_____

What are some action steps for moving out of broken cycles/self-talk of fear?

_____

_____

_____

_____

What life lessons have you learned about trading fear for your calling?

_____

_____

_____

Take Action with a Battle Plan

Every fear I had about my youngest daughter going to college started showing up her second semester in school. Influence of drugs by other students, attack to her self-worth, theft of her possessions, computer glitch dropping all her honors courses, unsafe spaces, hurt and frustration, health problems, and finally self-doubt tried to take up camp.

We had prayed Ephesians 3:20 for months leading up to her arrival on campus in August. We believed that our God would do exceedingly and abundantly for her physical safety and also for her mental and emotional stability. I saw God show up in a way that I had never seen Him in her before. As we embraced to say our good-byes for that first time in August, I could feel the tangible presence of the Holy Spirit's peace wash over the room and both of us. My daughter looked me right in the eye and said, "I am not afraid, Mom. I know I had my moments of panic on the journey to this moment, but I honestly don't have any fear in my heart. I know I can do this. I am ready." Her ability to verbalize the saturated peace I was feeling surrounding us in that moment grounded me in such a way that worship was all I could bring my soul to do. That a God who controls the universe would pause to touch the heart, mind, and spirit of _my little girl_ and His daughter just blew me away. Not a tear, not a fret … just a room consumed with love.

But here we were just four months later and spiritual warfare was moving in to take up shop. Through the text messages, tearful calls, and discouraged social media posts, I had to decide how I was going to respond to my fear and how my response would impact what my daughter grows to believe about fear.

Have you ever been there? You thought you had licked it, beat it, and put it in your back pocket as done. But life has a way of revealing what we *really believe* to be true. I realized in a lesson from activist, evangelist, and author Christine Caine that it will not be what you read or were taught about God that will sustain you in a trial. When trials hit, you will drop to whatever level of *revelation* you have about who God is in that moment, and that will be the place that you survive from. Yeah, what revelation did I have about who God is to me and who He is to my daughter? The fight was on, and I needed to know who was showing up in the battle with me.

EXODUS 14:13–14 (MSG) *Moses spoke to the people: "Don't be afraid. Stand firm and watch God do his work of salvation for you today.* **Take a good look at the Egyptians today for you're never going to see them again. God will fight the battle for you. And you? You keep your mouths shut!"**

The challenge is that if I get caught up in the fight, flight, or freeze mode of my response to a fear state, I lose sight of the ability to recall the weapons I have access to in the battle. Dr. Bruce Perry explains that at any given moment, we are in one of five brain states: Calm, Alert, Alarmed, Fearful, or Terror. Being at our creative peak places us in the state of Calm, but the lower we drop in our brain state, the less able we are to think clearly. In a state of Alert, we access concrete thinking, but when we drop into Alarmed, we become emotional thinkers. When we are Fearful, we become reactive in our thoughts. In a state of Terror, we are just reflexive in our thought patterns— flexing without even thinking.

God knows how He created our brains and how our minds respond, so He tells the Israelites as well as us to not even lower your state of mind into a place of fear or terror because that will interfere with your ability to think clearly when I give you the okay to move. Stand firm and become grounded and stable to remain fully engaged in the moment, because I need you to polish your lenses because you are getting ready to get a whole new revelation of who I am. So watch and see how your God will show up for you on this day.

Recalling 2 Timothy 1:7 challenged me in those moments with my daughter. Do I actually believe He did not give me the spirit of fear? So if fear isn't coming from God, who is it coming from? Satan. Our enemy! He is using a natural signal that God has given to be an alert to needs and allowing it to run roughshod over my life and attack my daughter. On no! We didn't come this far for some already defeated trickster and father of lies to have dominion over this or any other situation.

But wait … I'm physically 11 hours away from my daughter! What kind of attack plan can I have with the barriers of distance and time between us and *pharaoh's chariots* closing in on her? Stand firm! What does that look like? What had we prayed for months before she even left for school in the summer?

I recalled our prayers—that our God would show up in abundance in her life emotionally, physically, financially, academically, and spiritually. Hmmm. See any correlation to the attack listed above?

"Influence of drugs by other students, attack to her self-worth, theft of her possessions, computer glitch dropping all her honors courses, unsafe spaces, hurt and frustration, health problems, and finally self-doubt"!

Oh no, devil! Not on this watch. Greater is He within us than in the world. It is time to stand firm on the same battle plan we used to get us to this spot of favor in the first place

- Quiet our mind of fear by posting the truth of God's word everywhere, visibly in the house and car
- Stand firm in prayer and use the weapon of worship when the sensation of fear wants to creep back in
- Bear witness to the attack and God's faithfulness with a core group of believing accountability partners who will watch, pray, and encourage throughout the battle.

I went back to our Power Plan from pre-August prep. Because toxic emotions can flood our brains and disrupt memory, recall, and critical thinking, I had to create a visual card that reminded me of the battle strategies that were at my fingertips, internally and externally. We wrote down three things that we would do either internally or externally to bring us back to spiritual grounding when under emotional, mental, or spiritual attack. I reminded myself that when situations are out of my physical reach, they are never out of reach of God's hand. And I needed a visual reminder of how to fear not, stand firm, and watch the power of God. Adapted from Dr. Sandra Bloom's safety plan, these things became our coping strategies when we were flooded with emotions or thoughts that stemmed from things completely out of our control. For example, internal power strategies we listed could be used mentally or emotionally when no one else knew, such as repeating 2 Timothy 1:7 in our mind, saying a truth about God's character under our breath, and visually seeing a mental picture of grace. Some examples of external power strategies included things that people could physically see us using, such as singing praise and worship songs, taking three cleansing deep breaths to stabilize our heart and mind, walking and talking through scripture, and using a soft fidget to touch, squeeze, or hold to release tension from our body. Being intentional about creating and writing a visual Power Plan while we were calm and able to think allowed us to have a visual reminder in emotional moments when we were not able to think clearly. (For a free downloadable copy of "Your Belief Controls Your Behavior Power Plan," go to our website, https://livingstrongllc.com/fearlessly-free-downloads.)

I had to shut down the broken cycle of mental chatter created from a lack of control; tap into the love, power, and sound mind offered to me; and reckon with what I really *believed* about a God who had already shown Himself to be faithful. You see, these battles are not just about the pharaoh, his army, or my daughter's trials. They are about opening our eyes to God's ability to show up, save, and fight. Neither my hand nor the Israelites' hands could be on it, because God needed full credit. From the perspective of both scenarios, this became an opportunity to rewire the distorted neurological circuits twisted from years of slavery and to establish the fertile ground for the roots of my daughter's relationship with her God. It was about *revelation, not just rescue.* That's how you never see *this Egyptian* again. Because the revelation of who God is sets into your mind and shifts your entire view of how God can, will, and does show up in your life. It's not that the Israelites would never see another enemy again or that my daughter will never have moments of battle again, but that when we witness God's hand on a situation and see the aftermath of how He can handle the attack …

EXODUS 14:29–31 (NIV) *But the Israelites went through the sea on dry ground, with a wall of water on their right and on their left. That day the Lord saved Israel from the hands of the Egyptians, and Israel saw the Egyptians lying dead on the shore. And when the Israelites saw the mighty hand of the Lord displayed against the Egyptians, the people feared the Lord and put their trust in him and in Moses his servant.*

… the enemy never has to have the same amount of power over our emotions, mind, reactions, and state of being again, and we become fearless.

As Scripture says, what the devil meant for bad, God meant for good. On the other side of her battle plan, my daughter ended up posting Scripture and truth of her value all over her social media pages, so every young adult she was associated with could see her declaration and faith. Her teammates, coaches, and professors could see her strength and stability in struggle and her innate leadership ability. She witnessed a circle of women of God intercede in prayer, messages, and Scripture for her to remember she is not alone. And when your daughter sends you her worship music for the day—sharing that she is in "beast mode"—you just shake your head, smile, and say, "Yep, devil, not today!"

Check out our Pursuit Cards in our eStore for visual daily reminders of how to break broken patterns and live life to the fullest ... and running over ☺! https://gumroad.com/livingstrongllc#

Reflect on Your Growth

Take some time for focused reflection and intentional celebration.

Review your journal or notes from this chapter. What are your top three takeaways from this experience? Why did those things stand out to you?

_____

_____

_____

_____

Mind. Body. Soul. Connection: Now let's restore some mental pathways through the therapeutic activity of coloring. Take this time to connect worship, prayer, music, and stillness while you focus on the creative act of coloring. Coloring has been found to reduce anxiety, increase focus, build awareness, and provide clarity. When you take the time to calm your mind, your brain enters a relaxed state by focusing on the present and blocking out the nonstop thinking we all experience. As a result, you reach a place of calm that relieves your brain from the daily stresses of life and allows you to continue to refresh and restore. So find your favorite worship song and a quiet place to sit, and let's start coloring.

2 TIMOTHY 1:7 (NKJV) *For God has not given us a spirit of fear, but of power and of love and of a sound mind.*

Core Beliefs Shape Your Battle Plan

Basement: Do You Have Power or Not?

"I did not allow you to enter this battle because you are a worrier. You are in this battle because you are a Warrior!"—God

I want you to identify something that belongs to you, that is precious to you. Something that represents time, energy, money, relationship, or desires. How would you respond if I walked up to you and said, "I am taking that from you!" What would be some of your emotions or responses?

I know that trying to take something from you that you cherish, worked for, and wanted could start a fight. I wouldn't be able to get it out of your hands easily. Snatching something out of your grip would bring up some pretty big emotions and actions. Okay, okay, calm down. LOL. Just thinking about it gets me upset.

What I want you to understand from this demonstration is that every person, every life you impact by walking out your calling as a woman of God and that person is brought into the Kingdom—you have snatched them from the hand of Satan, and he has the same fight response. Even your act of wiggling out of his grip by getting your thought life in order, strengthening your faith, and shifting your perspective of fear raises strategic warfare in his response. He has invested time, energy, relationships, and desire in that life and any broken areas in your life that you are now prying from his grip. And he is mad.

Can I ask a question? If Satan has decided to destroy, can we decide to walk in destiny? I know we ask the question, "Why does this have to be so hard?" I have asked myself the same thing. Then the answer hit me: Stop believing the battle is supposed to be fair; a battle is never fair, easy, or without blows. How will you know for yourself that you are *more than* a conqueror if you have never fought through anything to conquer?

If you know you are in spiritual warfare, start fighting *for* your destiny and not *against* your destiny with the defeating belief that you deserve something easier. What if you just get *mad* that the enemy is hitting you and your destiny and stop expecting things to be fair and get up every day ready to fight? Shift your mindset. Accept the battle, because you don't enter it alone, and He is preparing you for what He has prepared for you. *Now fight for it!* People are depending on you to live your purpose. And God will get the glory.

I am not giving you this spiritual pep talk to discourage you or place fear in you. I am telling you this so that you *know* your enemy, because he *knows you,* but more importantly, *he knows the God in you!* Walking, living, and breathing this truth requires us to reckon with what we actually believe about the God in us and His ability to show up for us. When we hear verses like ...

PSALM 23:6 (NIV) *Surely your goodness and love will follow me all the days of my life, and I will dwell in the house of the Lord forever.*

... do we truly believe that in the heat of the battle, the goodness of God's character will show up, even if it does not look the same way we designed it in our heads? Entering into battle requires clarity and grounding in what we actually believe about the one we call Provider, Protector, Healer, and Way Maker. In truth, our enemy knows the power, character, and embedded victory of our God, but he depends on us not knowing it for ourselves to wreak havoc in our lives with traps, schemes, and battle plots that have us question our power and the power and faithfulness of our battle commander.

What do you believe?

Who is God?

_____

_____

_____

_____

_____

How does God show up in my life?

_____

_____

_____

_____

_____

_____

What can He do for me?

_____

_____

_____

_____

_____

What is His character like?

_____

_____

_____

_____

_____

What can I trust Him with?

_____

_____

_____

_____

_____

Fearless Conversations with a Limitless God

How does your daily life reflect the truth of what you just wrote down about God?

_____

_____

_____

_____

_____

Which areas of God's character do you struggle with to believe?

_____

_____

_____

_____

Our core belief is not formed by theory or teachings about God, but through experiences with God. Until we pause, integrate the teachings and instruction that we have heard, and reflect on God's presence in our lives—actually look for His fingerprints on situations—our perception of His character as a powerful, all-knowing, sovereign, trustworthy, and faithful God will be sprinkled with doubt.

Why does our enemy depend on that doubt?

_____

_____

_____

_____

Jesus reminds us that our speech and actions reveal our beliefs, attitudes, and motivations. The outward impressions, masked actions, or orchestrated phrases that we try to make cannot last if our hearts are confused. The lie or the truth we have hidden in our hearts will come out in our speech and behavior.

The mental health and family wellness team at Betterrelation ships.org defines core beliefs as "a basic belief about ourselves, other people, and the world we live in. They are the things we hold to be absolute truths deep down, underneath all our 'surface' thoughts. Essentially, core beliefs sit in the basement of your mind and determine how you perceive and interpret the world around you."

Although belief systems can change, it usually takes time and mental shifts in practice. The story we form from the lens through which we view our experiences impacts the story we tell ourselves daily. And when we allow our mind, body, and spirit to be flooded by emotions, it can create what Dena Rosenbloom and Mary Beth Williams, the authors of *Life after Trauma*, call "all-or-nothing thinking." When life events have given us a story to believe based on hurtful experiences, we can begin to believe it is self-protective to believe the extremes of being completely safe or completely unsafe, in complete control or completely out of control. This keeps us on guard and dependent on our own perception of what we can tangibly keep on hand and manipulate to ensure we control our fate. This limited view of our reality in a battle is why God offers us a breastplate of righteousness, as described in Ephesians 6:14 (NIV): *Stand firm then, with the belt of truth buckled around your waist, with the breastplate of righteousness in place.* This piece of armor Paul describes is meant to protect a warrior in battle by first being hinged to the belt of truth; without the belt of truth, the breastplate would fall off. With the image of a secure breastplate, the warrior is equipped to protect her heart. This gives us the opportunity to pause and really think about God's intentionality for protecting our place of emotions and felt value, which gives God the opportunity to paint the picture of offering us safety, not in our defenses alone but from His righteousness resting on the truth of His character. But the use of these parts of our armor is connected to our willingness to put them on. We must be willing to practice the daily rewriting of false truth and all-or-nothing thinking programmed by the enemy and refocus our lenses on the truth of what we have available to us to tap into the power of God's presence when He steps on the scene. No, things may not always look the way we want them to, but developing a continuum of our perspective on trusting God in the middle of the risk builds our daily process of preparing for the battle.

Awareness: Who's Got Your Back?

The power and anointing of the Holy Spirit is all over women of God, and our just entering the room sends Satan into a panic. Do we believe that? Paul's Prayer for the Ephesians and across generations for us as well paints such a clear picture of the power we have access to through the faithfulness of our God.

EPHESIANS 3:19–21 (NKJV) *… to know the love of Christ which passes knowledge; that you may be filled with all the fullness of God. Now to Him who is able to do exceedingly abundantly above all that we ask or think, according to the power that works in us, to Him be glory in the church by Christ Jesus to all generations, forever and ever. Amen.*

Satan knows what you have access to and who you are with. When will we *know* it, *believe* it, and *fight like we know it*?

Even if we don't realize when Jesus has stepped into the picture, Satan does, and he is quaking in his boots because he knows his defeat is already imminent—just because you and your Father have arrived together on the scene!

This truth plays out in a familiar story about a man and some pigs. We are going to unpack the truths of core belief and how they shift calling, purpose, and freedom in this familiar passage of Scripture.

At the start of the passage, Jesus and the disciples have just come out of a tremendous, life-threatening storm and have stepped on the shore of the Sea of Galilee. They are greeted by a man tortured by demons.

MARK 5:1–6 (KJV) *And they came over unto the other side of the sea, into the country of the Gadarenes. And when he was come out of the ship, immediately there met him out of the tombs a man with an unclean spirit, Who had his dwelling among the tombs; and no man could bind him, no, not with chains: Because that he had been often bound with fetters and chains, and the chains had been plucked asunder by him, and the fetters broken in pieces: neither could any man tame him. And always, night and day, he was in the mountains, and in the tombs, crying, and cutting himself with stones.* **But when he saw Jesus afar off, he ran and worshipped him.**

First truth. There's a quote from evangelist and author Priscilla Shirer that makes this passage resonate with me: "Satan is not God's counterpart … He is not His equal … He is not His evil twin." If we could just get clear on that. Satan and his demons know it. The moment Jesus stepped into the picture, a man who had been tortured by demons to the point where he could not live in society with others, broke chains and lived among the dead in a cemetery dropped in submission and fear at the feet of Jesus, acknowledging who He was and the power that He brings.

This image raises a fight in me. When I think of everything that the enemy has tried to torture me with and strip me of, just like our conversation at the start of this chapter, I realize he is intentionally trying to take something that belongs to me. When I decide and believe that the enemy will not take another thing from me, any demon who has plotted an attack on me shakes! It makes me stand, *believe*, and say, "I am who God has said I am. I will have *all* that He has promised me."

My mind
My peace
My calling
My voice
My dreams
My promises
BECAUSE HE LIVES IN ME, AND HE'S GOT MY BACK!

What has God promised you?

_____

_____

_____

_____

_____

MARK 5:4–8 (NLT) *Whenever he was put into chains and shackles—as he often was—he snapped the chains from his wrists and smashed the shackles. No one was strong enough to subdue him. Day and night he wandered among the burial caves and in the hills, howling and cutting himself with sharp stones.* **When Jesus was still some distance away, the man saw him, ran to meet him, and bowed low before him. With a shriek, he screamed, "Why are you interfering with me, Jesus, Son of the Most High God? In the name of God, I beg you, don't torture me!" For Jesus had already said to the spirit, "Come out of the man, you evil spirit."**

Why is this part of the passage significant? Because even from a far-off distance, the demons knew their fall was imminent! Just because Jesus stepped on the shore, on the scene. Just like the demons who have twisted your thinking, robbed you of peace, kept you up at night, wreaked havoc in your family, disrupted your office—they knew the end was coming, but sometimes we miss it.

You see, the demon knew something that the disciples who had been with Jesus did not know. In just the chapter before this one, they had been through storms with him and still asked, "Who is this man?" (Mark 4:41).

But this demon called Him by name when Jesus stepped on the shore: *"Why are you interfering with me, Jesus, Son of the Most High God? In the name of God, I beg you, don't torture me!" For Jesus had already said to the spirit, "Come out of the man, you evil spirit."* (Mark 5:8 NLT) But all of this happened while Jesus was *afar off.* Jesus had not said an actual verbal word yet. The demon ran to Him based on just His presence. His presence did all the speaking, and the demon knew he could not continue to occupy the same space with the powerful spirit of the Most High. When we arm ourselves with this truth, any demon assigned to torture our mind, body, or spirit is forced to his knees.

It is time to activate His power and His plan. The same power that brings a legion of Demons to their knees at the sight of our Lord from afar off is the same power that rises with you and in you every morning when you place your feet on the floor, when you stand before the board, when you must show love to that wayward child, when you step out to take a risk, when you choose to believe God's hope and not the facts of the doctor's note. Why is this significant? Because a double-minded, defeated, discouraged Christian who lacks peace and is miserable is no threat to the enemy. But a Christian who is ready to access the power of God through faith, joy, promise, growth, and truth is able to walk in the peace and confidence of fully understanding what the battle is actually about.

MARK 5:10–13 (NLT) *Then the evil spirits begged him again and again not to send them to some distant place. There happened to be a large herd of pigs feeding on the hillside nearby. "Send us into those pigs," the spirits begged. "Let us enter them." So Jesus gave them permission. The evil spirits came out of the man and entered the pigs, and the entire herd of about 2,000 pigs plunged down the steep hillside into the lake and drowned in the water.*

Why did the legion (a military term for a large number of soldiers) ask to be sent into the pigs? Verse 10 spells it all out for us. The evil spirits "begged Him again and again not to send them to some distant place." They didn't want to be out of the territory. The battle, torment, and struggle this man had been going through was not about him. They didn't ask to keep him, the man. They asked to keep the territory. A legion of demons had staked claim to the area and didn't want to let it go without a fight. Wow, this is a sobering truth for us. What we go through is not just about us, but about the territory we are assigned and given power to take in the name of our God. If the demons can prevent us from seeing this, we will sit in the "why me?" pity party of our lives instead of getting angry for being messed with, because Satan wants our stuff, our children, our territory, our ministry, our relationships, our influence.

What has Satan taken from your territory that you are going into battle to take back from him *today*?

_____

_____

_____

_____

_____

Why are you taking it back? Because it was promised to you, it belongs to you, and God has given you permission to *claim it*. The territory has been promised to you. **Joshua 1:3 (NLT)** *I promise you what I promised Moses: "Wherever you set foot, you will be on land I have given you."*

Understanding: Your Belief Controls Your Behavior

In October of 2017, my best friend, Tina Pelzer, had a stroke. She was a woman of God, on fire and in full attack mode—making assault to the enemy's plan—at the time of the stroke. Just months before, I had asked her to have coffee with me so that I could share something God had placed on my heart. You see, even doing what we think is right and fierce for God can become distorted and used as a weapon against us. As we sat in the coffeehouse, we talked strategically about what the real battle was that she was facing. To say she was burning the candle at both ends was an understatement. She would book two, three, or even four ministry events in one day, knowing any human could do only one or two. Resting on our love for each other, I took my friend's heart in my hands and, with the holy spirit's guidance, challenged her on where her trust laid. You see, we can sometimes become so busy for God we forget that His plan does not rest in our ability to hustle for resources, create networks, make appointments, or be on constant duty for Him. He has not called us to perfection or exhaustion for Him, but has asked us to co-labor with Him. But what we believe about Him showing up when needed is sometimes distorted by what we have developed a belief system around based on what humans have done to or not done for us in the past.

Tina and I walked through how believing that she cannot depend on man was running over into her busyness in ministry for God. The enemy had begun to use an attack on her heart and the truth about her trust in God through her very calling to bring her to a place of burnout, stress, an overworked schedule, and on-call duty. It was this place of utter fatigue that caused me to ask to have coffee that day. Even though it was all for ministry, the Holy Spirit had let me see where her nonstop schedule, self-imposed pressure, and never-enough demands were leading. At the end of our coffee chat, Tina agreed to slow down, but the damage and toll on her body had already begun. Within a month or so, in the middle of worship, she went down …

Part 1: Go to the Fearless Conversations with a Limitless God Video Companion at https://gumroad.com/livingstrongllc#. (Enter the discount code m88hm52 to access the video content for free.) Then watch our "Iron Sharpens Iron" Fearless Conversations video about Tina's stroke, her fight back, and the lessons she learned. Listen how she has allowed God to use her story to set many others free, much like the man tortured by demons but freed to be used.

Key to remember: We have a Divine Commander in Chief, and He has issued a battle plan, but it is not dependent on our ability as a soldier alone.

2 CORINTHIANS 10:3–6 (MSG) *The world is unprincipled. It's dog-eat-dog out there! The world doesn't fight fair. But we don't live or fight our battles that way—never have and never will. The tools of our trade aren't for marketing or manipulation, but they are for demolishing that entire massively corrupt culture. We use our powerful God-tools for smashing warped philosophies, tearing down barriers erected against the truth of God, fitting every loose thought and emotion and impulse into the structure of life shaped by Christ. Our tools are ready at hand for clearing the ground of every obstruction and building lives of obedience into maturity.*

After watching Tina's testimony, how can you reduce distractions and activate His power and His plan for your victory?

_____

_____

_____

_____

_____

_____

_____

_____

Part 2: Return to the Video Companion at https://gumroad.com/ livingstrongllc# to watch the next "Iron Sharpens Iron" Fearless Conversations video. Listen as these women share their life lessons on accessing their battle plans for a life well lived. Reflect on the answers to the questions below. What is God revealing to you about living well, getting clear about what you believe, and using that belief in your battle?

Why is Satan's attack so fierce on our core beliefs?

_____

_____

_____

_____

_____

What does Satan use in our everyday life to sabotage us and distract us from abundant living?

_____

_____

_____

_____

_____

How can telling our story turn the tables on Satan's plan? What is he actually after in any attack?

_____

_____

_____

_____

How do we activate His power and plan for our victory? What role do our belief systems play?

_____

_____

_____

_____

What has God equipped us with in this battle?

_____

_____

_____

_____

_____

Action Steps: He Taught Me How to Fight

Recognize that your story is important because *what you have gone through* and *what you are going through* is important. In the next passage of the story, the legion of demons has been removed, they have been cast over the side of the mountain, and this man who once lived among the dead, wrapped in chains, is now free and approaching Jesus.

MARK 5:18–20 (NLT) *As Jesus was getting into the boat, the man who had been demon possessed begged to go with him. But Jesus said, "No, go home to your family, and tell them everything the Lord has done for you and how merciful he has been." So the man started off to visit the Ten Towns of that region and began to proclaim the great things Jesus had done for him; and everyone was amazed at what he told them.*

Jesus used the story of the very thing that tortured this man to change the lives of many! He commanded the man to go and tell. He has also told you, as a woman of God, to go, to step out, to tell, but He is not sending you out empty-handed. He knows the battle that is in front of you. He has equipped you with weapons to fight with because he knows what He has called you to fight against.

But His weapons are not the usual ones we grab; He has given us specific ones.

The Word

Placing any story into context is vitally important, so we need to go back in Mark just ahead of the start of this story.

MARK 4:3541 (NLT) *Late that day he said to them, "Let's go across to the other side." They took him in the boat as he was. Other boats came along. A huge storm came up. Waves poured into the boat, threatening to sink it. And Jesus was in the stern, head on a pillow, sleeping! They roused him, saying, "Teacher, is it nothing to you that we're going down?" Awake now, he told the wind to pipe down and said to the sea, "Quiet! Settle down!" The wind ran out of breath; the sea became smooth as glass. Jesus reprimanded the disciples: "Why are you such cowards? Don't you have any faith at all?" They were in absolute awe, staggered. "Who is this, anyway?" they asked. "Wind and sea at his beck and call!"*

Jesus and the disciples had crossed over to the pagan side of the Sea of Galilee. The battle for the life of this pagan man and the lives of the residents of the Ten Town area started *afar off!* Before they even stepped on land. Jesus started his journey with the intention of going to the other side! And the enemy's storm to stop him—to halt His next step, to hinder the deliverance of others—started before He even got to His destination. It was a storm so severe that the disciples thought their lives were in danger. Even *before* the full purpose and intent of the trip were revealed, the storm started! Actually, the storm was allowed, not for the sake of Jesus (He knew who He was and where He was going), but for those watching Him. The disciples still did not understand who they were with and the power they had in their presence. This is clear in their response: "Who is this man? That the wind and the sea obey Him." The very power of God slept and stood next to them, and they were *not clear* about what they believed about who and what they had at their fingertips in the man named Jesus. That was, until the Word made flesh used the word to calm the very thing that devastated and filled them with fear!

Jesus spoke ... and He is still speaking to us today—through His Word, the Bible.

JOSHUA 1:8–9 (NLT) *Study this Book of Instruction continually. Meditate on it day and night so you will be sure to obey everything written in it. Only then will you prosper and succeed in all you do. This is my command—be strong and courageous! Do not be afraid or discouraged. For the LORD your God is with you wherever you go.*

Your first weapon in the battle is the Word of God. Use it daily to listen for instruction and insight about the layout of the battle and the command to quiet the storms of life.

Your Worship

Get still, because I want you to think about one of your hardest days. A day when you struggled. When you hurt. When you thought, *I can't do this anymore.* Think about that time, pause ...

Guess what? You are *still here!* Think about this: Activist, evangelist, and author Christine Caine says, "On your worst day, Satan could not take you out on his best day!" *You are still here!*

And you have the nerve to cultivate clarity on your belief systems and seek a battle plan for a life of purpose.

When Satan hits you with his best and you come back with a song of praise, he has *no answer for that!*

2 CHRONICLES 20:1–2, 18–24 (MSG) *Some time later the Moabites and Ammonites, accompanied by Meunites, joined forces to make war on Jehoshaphat. Jehoshaphat received this intelligence report: "A huge force is on its way from beyond the Dead Sea to fight you. There's no time to waste." Then Jehoshaphat knelt down, bowing with his face to the ground. All Judah and Jerusalem did the same, worshipping GOD. The Levites stood to their feet to praise GOD, the God of Israel; they praised at the top of their lungs! They were up early in the morning, ready to march into the wilderness of Tekoa. As they were leaving, Jehoshaphat stood up and said, "Listen Judah and Jerusalem! Listen to what I have to say! Believe firmly in GOD, your God, and your lives will be firm! Believe in your prophets and you'll come out on top!" After talking it over with the people, Jehoshaphat appointed a choir for GOD; dressed in holy robes, they were to march ahead of the troops, singing, Give thanks to GOD, His love never quits. As soon as they started shouting and praising, GOD set ambushes against the men of Ammon, Moab, and Mount Seir as they were attacking Judah, and they all ended up dead. The Ammonites and Moabites mistakenly attacked those from Mount Seir and massacred them. Then, further confused, they went at each other, and all ended up killed. As Judah came up over the rise, looking into the wilderness for the horde of barbarians, they looked on a killing field of dead bodies—not a living soul among them.*

Do you see the illustration God gives us in this passage? Your worship will confuse the enemy so much that your enemies will kill off themselves before you even engage in any physical sweat. Your strength is in your worship.

PSALM 9:1–2 (MSG) *I'm thanking you, God, from a full heart, I'm writing the book on your wonders. I'm whistling, laughing, and jumping for joy; I'm singing your song, High God.*

For the next week, pick a different praise song or worship medley to play at the start of your day. Let the words and the melody saturate your spirit first thing in the morning and carry a sweet fragrance into your day. Each morning, write down the song you picked and what God revealed to you between the lyrics.

Day 1: _____

Day 2: _____

Day 3: _____

Day 4: _____

Day 5: _____

Day 6: _____

Day 7: _____

Your Warrior Stance

Our battles are best fought from our knees. I want you to engage in a moment right now to grasp hold of what He has for you—and prepare your battle plan in prayer.

EPHESIANS 6:18–20 (AMP) *With all prayer and petition pray [with specific requests] at all times [on every occasion and in every season] in the Spirit, and with this in view, stay alert with all perseverance and petition [interceding in prayer] for all God's people. And pray for me, that words may be given to me when I open my mouth, to proclaim boldly the mystery of the good news [of salvation], for which I am an ambassador in chains. And pray that in proclaiming it I may speak boldly and courageously, as I should.*

Pray the promises of God. The promises of your inheritance. The promises of God I stand on are:

I am Able (Romans 5:3–5)

I am Defended (Romans 12:19)

I am Delivered (Psalm 34:17)

I am Loved (Isaiah 54:10)

I am Free (Galatians 5:1)

I am Protected (Exodus 14:14)

I am Strong (Isaiah 40:29)

I am Equipped (2 Thessalonians 1:11)

I am Not Alone (Isaiah 41:10)

Rest in Reflection: What Has God Revealed to You?

How can your responses and reactions change in situations with a greater assurance of your core belief?

_____

_____

_____

_____

_____

_____

Take some time for focused reflection and intentional celebration. Review your journal or notes from this chapter. What are your top three takeaways from this experience? Why did those things stand out to you?

_____

_____

_____

_____

_____

_____

Mind. Body. Soul. Connection: Now let's restore some mental pathways through the therapeutic activity of coloring. Take this time to connect worship, prayer, music, and stillness while you focus on the creative act of coloring. Coloring has been found to reduce anxiety, increase focus, build awareness, and provide clarity. When you take the time to calm your mind, your brain enters a relaxed state by focusing on the present and blocking out the nonstop thinking we all experience. As a result, you reach a place of calm that relieves your brain from the daily stresses of life and allows you to continue to refresh and restore. So find your favorite worship song and a quiet place to sit, and let's start coloring.

HEBREWS 6:1 (MSG) *So come on, let's leave the preschool finger painting exercises on Christ and get on with the grand work of art. Grow up in Christ. The basic foundational truths are in place: turning your back on "salvation by self-help" and turning in trust toward God.*

Stepping Out of the Hiding Places of Shame

Come Out of the Basement: How Does Shame Hold Us Back?

JOHN 4:7–10 (ESV) *A woman from Samaria came to draw water. Jesus said to her, "Give me a drink." (For his disciples had gone away into the city to buy food.) The Samaritan woman said to him, "How is it that you, a Jew, ask for a drink from me, a woman of Samaria?" (For Jews have no dealings with Samaritans.) Jesus answered her, "If you knew the gift of God, and who it is that is saying to you, 'Give me a drink,' you would have asked him, and he would have given you living water."*

In this story, we see a woman standing at the threshold of thirst looking into the opportunity for thriving. At first glance, you might not see it, but what actually happens here is a woman is offered release from shame, guilt, doubt, regret, defeat, and hurt. This sets her up for later in the story when she finds the strength to drop her cracked, limited past to reach for a fresh rejuvenation and opportunity to live in a new future.

But at this moment, she is at a threshold, and first, she must come out of *hiding* to accept the invitation in front of her. Now, when I talk about *hiding places,* I am referring to those broken memories, distorted beliefs, unforgiven heart hurts—those things that have been pushed down into hidden places within her and us. Our hiding places may not look the same as this woman's trip to the well, but we have our own hiding places today as well. An overbusy schedule, a Facebook page of amazing stories, another plate of food even when we are not really hungry, an overdrawn credit card, a smile painted on with the latest makeup products, our Sunday best, or a short-fuse response with every gesture of a friend or mate, the list could go on. All are examples of hiding places.

When we carry around baggage that we were never intended to carry—emotionally, physically, spiritually, or mentally—our brains push us into seeking out those hiding places. But let's be honest: Our God did not die on the cross, snatch death from the hand of the enemy, and rise with all power in his hand on the third day, guaranteeing victory over our lives, for us to be in hiding places! So let's unpack this story and walk out the process of how to move from being thirsty to transformed and then becoming a transformer.

The woman at the well arrived at a place in which she was thirsty. She may have shown up to that well with an empty bucket, but she was completely filled to the brim with shame and seeking the chance to hide from it at every turn. That's clear in her arrival at the middle of the day to retrieve water—a task usually reserved for the cool of morning hours. She knew that this time of day would better ensure she would not be seen, heard, or spoken to—perpetuating her isolation and validating her unworthiness. The lie of shame causes us to hide because in the deepest parts of ourselves, we're afraid that what *they* are saying about us and the broken pattern of what we think of ourselves *could be true*. So actually, we are not only hiding from our accuser; we're hiding from ourselves as well.

The devastating trick and damage of shame is wielded in the cloak of seclusion. If the enemy can get you alone and keep you alone, his plot in John 10:10 to kill, steal, and destroy has a playground to play in within our isolated thoughts and mind. So often, when we walk alone and rehearse the narrative of broken stories, hurts, and memories, we go on autopilot, playing these distorted self-narratives like an outdated mental playlist of hurt. This makes us choose coping strategies that help us survive the hurt by keeping us in a pattern of hiding or running, and when we do not share our emotional lives, closeness suffers and freedom is blockaded.

You see, shame is the feeling that there's something wrong with us that makes us unworthy of love. It makes us feel that we don't belong. Our Samaritan woman revealed this part of her broken narrative in her response to Christ by deflecting his initial *open engagement* with the closed defense of *"How is it that you, a Jew, ask for a drink from me, a woman of Samaria?" (For Jews have no dealings with Samaritans.)* Shame reduces our identity to the broken stories, stereotypes, and narratives that others place on our potential. But when we encounter our God just like this woman encountered Him, we are met at our place of thirstiness with Grace that gives us refreshed experiences. They open us up to be and do what destiny had already planned for us. But connecting with that refreshing experience, knowledge, and truth of that kind of Grace requires us to renew our minds. The enemy comes to attack your circumstances and your physical state and also your mental capacity. And shame is his weapon of choice.

The challenge becomes that we are often hindered from renewing our minds by the shackle of the shame that holds us back. Just like the isolating coping strategy used by this Samaritan woman, shame only really works when it remains in hiding places.

It is secrecy.

It is a broken playlist of self-talk that continues to play on repeat.

It is a lie that we continue to believe from a past hurt that never sees the light but actually grows and cultivates in the dark.

When shame is allowed to grow in those dark places, we continually stay in a brain state of fear, terror, worry, brokenness—and even unforgiveness. At its core, the root of shame creates an ingrained mental and physical experience that stimulates the parts of the brain that are activated during physical pain. That's why the enemy depends on the isolated experience of this uninterrupted cycle of pain throughout our system—in our minds and also throughout our entire bodies and cells. God has given us the gift of imagination to create, design, and innovate, but in the presence of shame, this same gift becomes a threat that is played out as distorted imagination and broken stories replaying the twisted plot of what we believe or don't believe is possible for *a woman like me.* Our brains adapt to hearing and seeing those broken images of our imagination and changes and conforms to the story line. This cycle of activated pain and shame becomes our normal, and our bodies adapt to survive the crisis state our minds have placed them in. It is forced to adapt to a chemical response that should be reserved for fleeting moments of fight, flight, or freeze but has become a toxic everyday cycle of chemical release impacting our ability to think, breathe, eat, sleep, and live fully. As a result, we look up and find ourselves sick and stuck—stuck in routines that leave us thirsty, broken, and alone.

Like this Samaritan woman, we too can arrive at the well, as usual, carrying our pot filled with the patterns, habits, and expectations of "not enough," discounting our worth and mentally forecasting disaster, but little did she or we know that today was going to be the last day of playing broken stories in our minds. *This* divine appointment at the well would rewrite the script she was telling herself and the one we are replaying, and also the script to the next chapters of our lives.

"Call out" the things in your thought life that are old and are no longer benefiting the new direction you are going in. On a separate piece of paper, create a "Same Old Thing" list, and each time a moment of fear creeps up, write down the lie that the fear is wrapped in, and then say the verse 2 Corinthians 5:17 (MSG) out loud to yourself: "Therefore, if anyone is in Christ, the new creation has come: The old is gone, the new is here!" When you are done with the same old thing list, look at the lies that are no longer your truth and throw them away.

Now it's time to detox your mind. Whatever we allow to captivate our thought life will eventually control our lives. *Pay attention* to your self-talk. *Practice* talking about the life you want to have. (Complaining is a trap.) *Plan* how you will be an influence for others and become purpose driven. What would an abundant life look like for you? *Write down* things that describe this life. Then post it to shift your focus.

Practice: _____

_____

Plan: _____

_____

Describe: _____

_____

_____

Step Into Awareness: Gain Clarity and Truth about Christ's Reaction to Shame

JOHN 4:7–18 (ESV) *A woman from Samaria came to draw water. Jesus said to her, "Give me a drink." (For his disciples had gone away into the city to buy food.) The Samaritan woman said to him, "How is it that you, a Jew, ask for a drink from me, a woman of Samaria?" (For Jews have no dealings with Samaritans.)* **Jesus answered her, "If you knew the gift of God, and who it is that is saying to you, 'Give me a drink,' you would have asked him, and he would have given you living water."**

The woman said to him, "Sir, you have nothing to draw water with, and the well is deep. Where do you get that living water? Are you greater than our father Jacob? He gave us the well and drank from it himself, as did his sons and his livestock." Jesus said to her, "Everyone who drinks of this water will be thirsty again, but whoever drinks of the water that I will give him will never be thirsty again. The water that I will give him will become in him a spring of water welling up to eternal life." The woman said to him, "Sir, give me this water, so that I will not be thirsty or have to come here to draw water." Jesus said to her, "Go, call your husband, and come here." The woman answered him, "I have no husband." Jesus said to her, "You are right in saying, 'I have no husband'; for you have had five husbands, and the one you now have is not your husband. What you have said is true."

In His humanness, tied to His divinity, Jesus already understood what she had been going through. Because His love had knit her worth together in her mother's womb, He was clear that the parchedness He recognized in her desperate steps as she approached the well was not the cadence He had planned for her. It was finally time for her to put down the ways she had tried to deal with her shame and meet Christ with a well of grace that would change everything. He didn't hit her with theology and rules. Without using that tone of judgment she was used to hearing from others, He went immediately for the root of her issues, not to condemn her but to free her from her secrecy and isolation through grace, relationship, and revelation of the opportunity to be free. Romans 6:14 shares that *For sin shall not*

have dominion over you, for you are not under law but under grace.
Unlike the law she tried to use to push away from Christ earlier in their conversation, Jesus was using relationship and grace to pull her into the truth of who she was beyond what had happened to her.

Today was going to change the script on every routine she was used to. She wasn't sure of the *living water* that was being offered, but she was sure that she wanted to break the routine of needing to return to the same place every day—repeating the same patterns that left her thirsty, physically and emotionally, over and over again. Throughout Scripture, Christ has a way of disrupting expectations and routines. He becomes available by listening, believing, and touching the exploited places in the lives of others. He creates a safe place for her and us to become aware of and modify our current condition. He will not allow us to settle for needing to repeat our past patterns—returning to a well that will only lead us to becoming thirsty again. But He will challenge us to look at our coping strategies and reckon them with our current story to reconcile to a life set up for abundance. A life of shame will often have us act out patterns of brokenness in our relationships, our self-care, our health, or our behaviors. In order for Christ to refresh this Samaritan woman with living water, He needed to expose what was keeping her in hiding and thus in brokenness. By engaging her story, He made her aware of the stagnation of the water she was carrying with her from her past. He exposed her story and had her admit to herself that she was thirsty.

At first glance, you might think Jesus called her out and added to her shame, but actually He was confirming her truth and releasing the weight of her secrets. This woman has often been portrayed as some type of harlot, but I'd like to shed a different light on what may have been at the root of her pain: rejection and insecurity, not infidelity. During that time, women did not have the power to pick and choose their mates, to go in and out of relationships at will. Unlike some of today's portrayals of her as a fast woman of the night, Jesus was exposing, acknowledging, and accepting her truth of rejection. Each one of those men represented a time of rejection and abandonment for her, and the one she was with now did not value her enough to even marry her. Remember, men could have multiple wives at this time, so he could have brought her into his home, but for whatever reason, he had not. Jesus met her right in the middle of her shame and rejection. Instead of whispering behind her back, He met her at her deepest pain and said, "I know your story, and I am here anyway." Wow! What love and grace!

Remember earlier when I described how shame creates a chemical reaction in the brain and body that activates the regions of the brain that replicate pain? And I described how, in isolation, that cycling of pain runs uninterrupted and wreaks havoc on our mind, body, and life balance? Because our God knit us together with intention, the presence of love and social connection physically creates a counterattack to this toxic cycle. The presence of love decreases the activation of our fear response system. It tells that fight, flight, or freeze response part of our brain to "stand down." Love releases us from scanning the world around us for constant threat and disrupts our inner world from cycling shame. Shame cannot stand up in the presence of a social connection of empathy, understanding, and love. In that social arena, it is called out for the lie that it is and placed on notice of its upcoming demise. Love physically activates the reward systems in our brain and releases restorative chemical responses throughout our body and cells. Love turns off threat and alarm, cancels our insecurities, and frees us from worry.

In an encounter of Acceptance, Transparency, and Love with our Christ, a woman hindered by rejection and thirsty from a life of shame began to step out of the shadows into the light. Into her purpose. Into her truth. And Christ would transform her truth into her worship.

In what area(s) of your life would you like to experience freedom in Christ?

_____

_____

_____

_____

_____

_____

Explore Understanding: What Shame-Based Habits Are You Dropping Because They No Longer Serve You?"

JOHN 4:11–18 (ESV) *The woman said to him, "Sir, you have nothing to draw water with, and the well is deep. Where do you get that living water? Are you greater than our father Jacob? He gave us the well and drank from it himself, as did his sons and his livestock." Jesus said to her, "Everyone who drinks of this water will be thirsty again, but whoever drinks of the water that I will give him will never be thirsty again. The water that I will give him will become in him a spring of water welling up to eternal life." The woman said to him, "Sir, give me this water, so that I will not be thirsty or have to come here to draw water." Jesus said to her, "Go, call your husband, and come here." The woman answered him, "I have no husband." Jesus said to her, "You are right in saying, 'I have no husband'; for you have had five husbands, and the one you now have is not your husband. What you have said is true."*

"Sir," the woman said, "I can see that you are a prophet. Our ancestors worshiped on this mountain, but you Jews claim that the place where we must worship is in Jerusalem."

"Woman," Jesus replied, "believe me, a time is coming when you will worship the Father neither on this mountain nor in Jerusalem. You Samaritans worship what you do not know; we worship what we do know, for salvation is from the Jews. Yet a time is coming and has now come when the true worshipers will worship the Father in the Spirit and in truth, for they are the kind of worshipers the Father seeks. God is spirit, and his worshipers must worship in the Spirit and in truth." The woman said, "I know that Messiah" (called Christ) "is coming. When he comes, he will explain everything to us."

Then Jesus declared, "I, the one speaking to you—I am he."

Christ did not wait for her to fit into a certain type of mold before meeting her at the well for a conversation. In fact, He took the ritual or routine she was trying to place Him in (*"Sir," the woman said, "I can see that you are a prophet. Our ancestors worshiped on this mountain, but you Jews claim that the place where we must worship is in Jerusalem."),* as a distraction from the real issues He was trying to address and completely dismantled it. Often, we repeat rituals, routines, patterns, thoughts, and behaviors because they have become habits. They become so much a part of us that they become unconscious. As we create behaviors, the brain creates a neuropathway for them, and over time that pathway turns into a three-lane concrete highway. It behaves like a high-speed, automatic response system that we are unaware of because the response is now our normal and is unconsciously completed because it is comfortable—even if that comfort is short-lived, is unhealthy, or keeps us hidden from our full potential. The patterned habit, thought, or behavior may feel good …

The blowup felt good in the moment …

That angry disconnect gave the pleasure of revenge for the moment …

That one more sweet treat felt good going down for the moment …

The silent treatment may have felt good in the moment …

The decision to not forgive may seem to give you comfort in the moment.

Likewise, as the Samaritan woman settled in her comfort zone, her decision to isolate herself from others may have created the deception of comfort. That pattern deceives us because it is freely flowing on a neurological highway created by a past path of brokenness.

Even though the Samaritan woman's story has been exposed by Jesus when he brings up the topic of her husband (in verses John 4:16–18), in an effort to protect the comfort of her patterns, rituals, and routines, she tries to distract Jesus from digging any deeper into her pain by pointing to a pattern of worship that had become comfortable for Jew and Gentile. In John 4:19–20, she tries to shift the issue from her personal thirst to the task of worship. But Jesus brings her right back to the root of her need again. He challenges her with the idea that worship is not about the ritual, tradition, or location that it occurs in, but rather about the heart that it occurs in. He takes hold of another thirsty place and uses it to draw her in. He didn't want to affect just her location of worship, but her life in worship.

Dismantling the concept of worship being a place or a program, He offered her an opportunity to move from playing out a familiar pattern in her head to showing up in a truth of who she could be as a worshipper *in spirit and in truth*. This shift was breaking patterns that had provided her comfort but kept her from being free to be authentic and true. This invitation was creating access to worship in body and also in her spirit and soul. And what He reveals to her and us in this moment is that submitting to this truth requires her to come out of hiding and meet the needy thirst in relationship that we all have, and it is not "out there" somewhere, but right in front of us, in Christ. The Greek word Christ uses for truth in this passage is *aletheia*, which means unclosedness or unconcealedness. The literal meaning of the word is "a state of not being hidden." Christ is informing her that true worship is not about the physical place where we stand, but the spiritual openness and uncovered state of our being as we come out of hiding to engage with Him in all that we authentically are for Him to have access to all we can be.

Just as Christ created the opportunity for this woman through His engagement, now it is time for us to ask ourselves, "Does the pattern I have on autopilot actually bring me comfort, health, and wholeness, and if so, for how long?" Our God promises us life—life in abundance and life eternally. But to access that wholehearted living, we are required *to come out of hiding and leave the water jar that is no longer serving us* (John 4:28).

Go to the Fearless Conversations with a Limitless God Video Companion at https://gumroad.com/livingstrongllc#. (Enter the discount code m88hm52 to access the video content for free.) Then watch our "Iron Sharpens Iron" Fearless Conversations video. Listen as these women share their personal stories of pain, victory, and revelation, and then answer the following questions. What is God revealing to you about conquering the cycle of shame?

How does the weight of shame impact you physically?

_____

_____

_____

_____

_____

What do we need to be aware of in the cycle of shame?

_____

_____

_____

_____

_____

_____

How do we acknowledge our broken habits?

_____

_____

_____

_____

What is God revealing to you about habits that are no longer serving you in a life of abundance?

_____

_____

_____

_____

_____

_____

How can telling our story turn the mess of shame into the message of significance?

_____

_____

_____

_____

_____

What are some action steps for moving out of shame that you want to incorporate into your life today?

_____

_____

_____

_____

_____

_____

What life lessons have you learned about trading shame for the significance God offers us?

_____

_____

_____

_____

_____

_____

Take Clear Action: Why Must the Change Happen Now?

JOHN 4:25–26 ... *The woman said, "I know that Messiah (called Christ) is coming. When he comes, he will explain everything to us."*
Then Jesus declared, "I, the one speaking to you—I am he."

JOHN 4:28–31 ... *Then, leaving her water jar, the woman went back to the town and said to the people, "Come, see a man who told me everything I ever did. Could this be the Messiah?" They came out of the town and made their way toward him.*

JOHN 4:39–42 (NIV) ... *Many of the Samaritans from that town believed in him because of the woman's testimony, "He told me everything I ever did." So when the Samaritans came to him, they urged him to stay with them, and he stayed two days. And because of his words many more became believers.*

They said to the woman, "We no longer believe just because of what you said; now we have heard for ourselves, and we know that this man really is the Savior of the world."

Just like the Samaritan woman, we arrive in the presence of Christ thirsty. Our thirst can be met, but our stories don't stop there. You see, it was a mistake in thinking that buying this book was about you getting *just* your thirst met. It is also about being a vessel for meeting the thirst of others. Christ wanted the Samaritan woman to be refreshed and quenched so that her cadence changed, her countenance became rejuvenated, and she was strong enough to *go!* And He wants the same for each of us.

So often when I engage in this conversation, women ask, "Go where?" Then they confess, "I don't really know where God wants me to go, what my purpose is, or how it could possibly happen."

This is the equation people so often start with:

WHAT + HOW = IMPACT

Yes, UNAPOLOGETICALLY, speak your *What*. What do you want to do?

Say it! Write it!

This first step of being bold enough to say *What* we want often requires us to find quiet space to write it down.

So get quiet. What is He whispering to you? What has He *been* telling you?

_____

_____

_____

_____

_____

If you are still struggling with this step, don't worry. Many people do. It sometimes requires us to do **two things:**

First, stop replaying broken stories in your mind. (Renew your mind.)

Create three columns on a piece of paper, and for the next seven days, pay attention to your thought life.

Column 1: When a painful thought, broken narrative, or adopted lie enters your self-talk, write it in column 1.

(example) "I failed at that again!"

Column 2: Write what meaning have you placed on that statement?

(example) "I am not enough. My mistakes and failures reflect my lack of worth. My value is placed in what I do."

Column 3: How can you rewrite that distorted meaning in your mind? What truth can you replace that lie with? What affirmation can you begin to tell yourself *every time* that painful thought or self-talk rises up?

(example) "I am accepted by an intimate God who loves me beyond my faults and has equipped me for great things."

Action plan: For every painful thought or broken narrative, write an affirmation and repeat it daily to yourself. Here is an example of an affirmation written by one of our Fearless Conversations authors and participants, Deb Studevan.

A.C.C.E.P.T.E.D
by Deb Studevan

- I will be *Authentic* by loving and embracing the woman I see in the mirror without apology or compromise.

- I will be *Conscientious* to care well for self—emotionally, mentally, physically, and spiritually.

- I will be *Compelled* to achieve greatness—it's my destiny. "Being confident of this, that he who has begun a good work in you (me) will perform it until the day of Jesus Christ" (Philippians 1:6).

- I will be *Excited* about tests and trials that will strengthen my faith, which is more precious than gold (1 Peter 1:7).

- I will be *Prayerful* and give thanks to God in all situations (1Thessalonians 5:18).

- I will be willing to share my *Testimony* of God's faithfulness.

- I will *Endure* this journey of life with joy and assurance understanding that I will experience trouble, yet God has already overcome the world (John 16:33.)

- I will *Devote* my life to serving God and empowering women to live a brave, free, healed and fulfilled life in Christ.

Second, stop getting paralyzed by *How* your *What* could possibly happen. Actually, the equation on page 60 sets you up for not being able to think clearly about what you want.

Worrying about *How* something is going to work out paralyzes people. Most often, this is because we cannot figure out *how something could possibly work out*. Well, guess what? In the hands of a God who has already worked out the perfect plan, the *How* is none of your business (Jeremiah 29:11).

"For I know the plans I have for you, declares the LORD, plans for welfare and not for evil, to give you a future and a hope."

"I" (God), not "you": The impact He wants to do through you is bigger than you. Therefore, knowing the *How* is bigger than you too. There are *Hows* that haven't even been created yet that will be used as a catapult to your vision.

It is more important to get clear about **What** you want and **Why** it is necessary for you and those around you, and let God handle the **How**.

Who is waiting for you to come out of hiding, to stop the broken patterns that hinder you, to begin writing down what God has already been whispering to you and fear has kept you from acknowledging?

WHY + WHAT = EFFECTIVE IMPACT

JOHN 4:28–31 … *Then, leaving her water jar, the woman went back to the town and said to the people, "Come, see a man who told me everything I ever did. Could this be the Messiah?" They came out of the town and made their way toward him.*

What would have made a woman drop a pot that she arrived with, that she thought she needed, to run back and expose herself to the very people she was hiding from? She realized this experience was not just about her or just for her. She knew there were other *thirsty* people who needed to experience the refreshed transformation she had encountered in a conversation with Christ. She had encountered acceptance, transparency, and love, which pulled her out of hiding into a place of purpose. No longer hindered by rejection and shame, her *Why* became the priority and the process for others to be healed.

Why must your What happen now?

_____

_____

_____

_____

_____

_____

_____

Now, let's try again. What would an abundant life look like for you?

_____

_____

_____

_____

_____

_____

You have written down what an abundant life looks like for you and why it must happen, so spend time writing a mission statement for your life. Begin to focus on describing what you want to accomplish, what you want to contribute, and upon what you want to focus your actions, energy, and time.

Start with "I will…"

_____

_____

_____

_____

_____

_____

_____

Check out our Pursuit Cards in our eStore for visual daily reminders of how to break broken patterns and live life to the fullest … and running over! https://gumroad.com/livingstrongllc#

Rest in Reflection: What Has God Revealed to You?

Take some time for focused reflection and intentional celebration. Review your journal or notes from this chapter. What are your top three takeaways from this experience?

_____

_____

_____

_____

_____

_____

_____

Why did those things stand out to you?

_____

_____

_____

_____

_____

_____

Mind. Body. Soul. Connection: Now let's restore some mental pathways through the therapeutic activity of coloring. Take this time to connect worship, prayer, music, and stillness while you focus on the creative act of coloring. Coloring has been found to reduce anxiety, increase focus, build awareness, and provide clarity. When you take the time to calm your mind, your brain enters a relaxed state by focusing on the present and blocking out the nonstop thinking we all experience. As a result, you reach a place of calm that relieves your brain from the daily stresses of life and allows you to continue to refresh and restore. So find your favorite worship song and a quiet place to sit, and let's start coloring.

1 PETER 5:6–11 (MSG) *So be content with who you are, and don't put on airs. God's strong hand is on you; he'll promote you at the right time. Live carefree before God; he is most careful with you.* **Keep a cool head. Stay alert. The Devil is poised to pounce, and would like nothing better than to catch you napping. Keep your guard up. You're not the only ones plunged into these hard times. It's the same with Christians all over the world. So keep a firm grip on the faith. The suffering won't last forever. It won't be long before this generous God who has great plans for us in Christ—eternal and glorious plans they are!—will have you put together and on your feet for good. He gets the last word; yes, he does.**

ISAIAH 50:7 (ESV) *But the Lord God helps me; therefore I have not been disgraced; therefore I have set my face like a flint, and I know that I shall not be put to shame.*

Fix Your Focus on Faith

Step Out of the Basement:
When Fear Knocks on the Door, Let Faith Answer.

HAVE YOU EVER BEEN TO the Grand Canyon? I have, and frankly, I believe there should be railings! Wow, what a drop! Do you know why they tell people in high places to not look down? Because whatever you focus on *pulls you*. The same thing is true in life with our thoughts, self-talk, and words. When fear shows up, when we focus on it, repeat it, and rehearse it, it pulls us. It consumes us and oftentimes shifts our awareness of everything else.

Let's look at a passage of Scripture on faith and perspective.

2 KINGS 6:14–16 (NIV) *Then he sent horses and chariots and a strong force there. They went by night and surrounded the city. When the servant of the man of God got up and went out early the next morning, an army with horses and chariots had surrounded the city. "Oh no, my lord! What shall we do?" the servant asked. "Don't be afraid," the prophet answered. "Those who are with us are more than those who are with them."*

In this excerpt of scripture, the prophet Elisha is under attack for being obedient. He had been an instrument of defeat in the life of the King of Syria. Every time the king planned something, Elisha would hear from God and know the plan and head it off. So at this point in the story, the King of Syria has set a plot to kill Elisha and sends his great army to seize and destroy him.

That word *destroy* reminds me of another enemy that many of us may be familiar with in our daily lives. **John 10:10 (CEB)** *"The thief enters only to steal, kill, and destroy. I came so that they could have life—indeed, so that they could live life to the fullest."* We have an enemy that desires to do the same thing that the King of Syria sought for Elisha. But also like Elisha, each of us has been handpicked for an assignment by God, and in His hands we can be used as an instrument of defeat to any attack planned by our adversary.

Recognizing the attack strategy placed against us requires us to be sober in our thinking and attuned to the tricks and schemes of our enemy. 1 Peter 5:8 (ESV) explains, *Be sober-minded; be watchful. Your adversary the devil prowls around like a roaring lion, seeking someone to devour.* Have you ever felt consumed by fear? Almost like it was devouring your thoughts and mind? Toxic emotions have a powerful impact that can feel like they are engulfing us. Our enemy knows that power of unbridled emotions, and he often wields them as a weapon to our thought life, our focus, and our ability to actually see what we have access to. An unfortunate truth that we often miss in the middle of an emotional battle is that emotions lie. Also, our enemy uses the foundation of his character to distort the truth of where our eyes should refocus. **John 8:44 (ESV)** *"You are of your father the devil, and your will is to do your father's desires. He was a murderer from the beginning, and has nothing to do with the truth, because there is no truth in him. When he lies, he speaks out of his own character,* *for he is a liar and the father of lies."* The devil will use whatever tactic is available. Yes, he will also use our own emotions and our thoughts to lie to us. Emotions will change and flow with every turn of perspective, interaction, or shift in climate or mood. Just because our emotions deliver a thought to our mind does not mean that the thought is true.

God has given us the gift of being able to stop and separate His truth from emotional lies. It is called the act of metacognition. It's the act of thinking about what we are thinking about. It's pausing and taking captive the rebel thought or emotion and also taking account of what meaning that emotion, physical sensation, and idea has for us. How we respond to the challenges in front of us is not just about the facts of the situation but what those facts mean based on our past experiences.

Elisha's servant had probably heard or seen what happens to those attacked by the Syrian army. Based on his past experience of the aftermath from this king's threatening character, from his perspective, they had few options and were doomed. The imprint of his past experiences on his emotional memories took charge and got into the driver's seat of his perspective of possibilities. But, even when we know the basic facts of a situation and can agree on their details, we may not all agree on what they mean. Consider the following two perspectives. Which castaway is saved?

Castaway 1: If you are on a desert island feeling trapped by the sand around you, the sight of an approaching tiny boat might have you leap for joy at the thought of being rescued or saved.

Castaway 2: If you are on that tiny boat and you have been tossed by the waves of the sea and have felt trapped by the endless horizon of rocky currents, the sight of a desert island is an oasis of stability that fills you with the joy of being saved from being trapped by the water.

The meaning of safe for you depends on your perspective.

If you are on a desert island, feeling trapped by the sand around you, an approaching boat is an oasis to freedom. If you have been tossed by the waves of the sea and feel trapped by the current, the sight of land is an oasis of safety and stability. The meaning of *safe* for you depends on your perspective. The perspective you bring to the situation, your expectations, and what you are carrying with you from your past will impact your interpretation of what it means to be saved. Being able to move from overwhelmed to empowered by managing our thought life is our birthright. Taking intentional steps of not repeating emotional patterns and perspectives requires the practice of taking captive our thoughts (2 Corinthians 10:5) and accepting responsibility for what we are thinking (Proverbs 23:7). When we feel pulled by emotional memories that distort our perspective, metacognition makes us more aware of our thoughts and also allows us to change them. God would not instruct us to lay captive and do something that he has not given us the ability to do—process thoughts and also lay hold of them and change them and the behaviors that come with them. So in those moments of toxic thoughts and emotions, **Pause**, **Process**, and **Plan** for change of toxic thoughts and emotions:

1. Pay attention to the sensations you feel in your body when the repeated emotions and responses are triggered by the person, place, thing, or situation.
2. What do you feel—in your head and also in your body, such as a headache, stomach pain, light-headedness, flushed face, and racing heart—when triggered? Pay attention and write it down. **Become a detective to your own self-awareness.**
3. Ask yourself, "Why is this (person, place, thing, or situation) creating this reaction in me?"
4. Ask yourself, "What lie am I believing from my past experience that is showing up now in this reaction. (For example, I am guilty. I am not worthy. It is my fault. I am not enough. I cannot forgive.)
5. Ask yourself, "Is this thought or emotion working for me? Will this repeated emotional memory or idea help me reach my goal of abundant living?"
6. **Enter into a conversation with God through His word and prayer.** What does God say about this situation and about me? Find Scriptures and write them down.
7. What needs to be changed?
8. After you have evaluated the thought, ask yourself, "What do I want to do differently next time?"

Processing your thoughts, emotions, and memories is not an event. It is a journey. You will need to repeat this process over and over again as you become more and more aware of yourself, your body, your thoughts, and your enemy. It is a commitment to being intentional, consistent, and patient.

Write some thoughts or emotions that came up for you in the moment.

_____

_____

_____

Building Your Awareness: Shift Your Focus

2 KINGS 6:14–16 (NIV) *Then he sent horses and chariots and a strong force there. They went by night and surrounded the city. When the servant of the man of God got up and went out early the next morning, an army with horses and chariots had surrounded the city. "Oh no, my lord! What shall we do?" the servant asked. "Don't be afraid," the prophet answered. "Those who are with us are more than those who are with them."*

We must become fully aware of how the cycle of toxic emotions distorts our perspective to move forward in confidence and clarity about our identity, role, and use by God. When we are fully alert to who we are and who is with us, we are able to remain focused on what God will do through us, not what the enemy will do to us. Our very unyielding presence becomes a smack in the face of the enemy, just because we won't buckle to the emotional lies and won't quit. After everything we have been through, we're still here. After the divorce, the death, the betrayal, the hurt, the job loss, the _____. You fill in the blank. You and I are still here—here in the physical sense and also "here" emotionally, spiritually, and mentally, seeking more instruction from a conversation with God. We're getting equipped to fight the next battle even stronger.

The enemy has sent an army to distract, seize, and rattle us. So often, the reality of the details in our lives have us so zeroed in on the plot and schemes the enemy has set that fear rushes through our mind and runs on autopilot. Our eyes become so focused on the facts of what our stories may look like. Like Elisha's servant in this passage, we are certain, based on the facts of what happened, about the pending outcome. But God is calling us to not just zero in on the facts of the circumstance but to open our eyes to the spiritual truth of how He remains an ever constant presence in our lives.

God wants us to focus our lens on who is with us in the battle and the power that relationship possesses to ensure that regardless of temporary circumstance, our final position is one of "more than a conqueror." In verse 15, Elisha's servant was focused on the problem at hand. He spoke to and about the problem. He spent time worrying about the problem. As a result, the problem became the only reality he could see.

Now we can't fault Elisha's servant for his initial response. As human beings, we are wired to be biased about the negative. Have you ever had the words of one negative comment haunt you for days, even with friends surrounding you with words of affirmation? Have you heard of someone who continues to struggle with painful thoughts that they just can't shake from stinging criticism hurled at them decades before? I'll talk about myself: I have spoken to crowds of hundreds of women and been hugged and encouraged by their words of appreciation for God's gift in my presentation, yet one fleeting less than favorable comment from a passerby will run through my head from the platform to the parking lot. The reasoning behind this mental phenomenon is the very reason why Elisha would not let his servant sit in that moment of downward cycle. He grabbed a moment to pull his servant from focusing on the natural and open his eyes to the supernatural. We are wired to get stuck on the negative. It is a survival strategy that we have used since the exit from the Garden of Eden. At that point, to keep us out of harm's way, our brains needed to become wired to notice the negative, the bad, and the dangerous more readily than the good, because we depended on that wiring to survive. But that natural tendency to focus on the possible danger in life-threatening situations carries over into all areas of our lives. We naturally zero in on dangerous or threatening situations to better ensure that we are not harmed physically, emotionally, and mentally.

Yet this story in Scripture gives a practical example of how to respond to that hardwiring with a spiritual truth. Elisha locked into a spiritual truth that is reinforced in **Ephesians 6:12 (ESV)** *For we do not wrestle against flesh and blood, but against the rulers, against the authorities, against the cosmic powers over this present darkness, against the spiritual forces of evil in the heavenly places.* So, in an intimate conversation with his God, Elisha prayed that his servant's perspective shift from flesh and blood to spiritual forces.

2 KINGS 6:14–17 (NIV) *Then he sent horses and chariots and a strong force there. They went by night and surrounded the city. When the servant of the man of God got up and went out early the next morning, an army with horses and chariots had surrounded the city. "Oh no, my lord! What shall we do?" the servant asked. "Don't be afraid," the prophet answered. "Those who are with us are more than those who are with them."* **And Elisha prayed, "Open his eyes, Lord, so that he may see." Then the Lord opened the servant's eyes, and he looked and saw the hills full of horses and chariots of fire all around Elisha.**

It's important to take note of Elisha's response to his servant. He didn't say, "Let him go fight, Lord, with great might!" He knew the greater issue wasn't the battle raging around them but the clouded battle coursing through him. The real threat was not flesh and blood. It was in the spiritual realm, in what his servant believed. In that moment, it was more necessary to shift his faith. This battle was not going to be the last fight in his life, so Elisha knew his servant needed a shift in his perspective and understanding of how committed God is to every promise He has mapped out for him. How He is already ahead of him in the midst of the problem creating the way out of no way. These moments in Scripture provide the chance for us, just like Elisha's servant, to see God and His power for ourselves. Elisha didn't just tell him about the horses and chariots of fire and ask the servant to trust him at his word for what he could see. No, he had a conversation with God that He would open the servant's spiritual eyes, his eyes, and his revelation of God for himself. The servant could no longer depend on Elisha's understanding of God's grace, mercy, and power. It was time for his own revelation, because for the next battle that arises it will be this moment of personal revelation and rewired emotional memories of this saving power known by the servant that will fortify his own faith and elevate him for the next plateau of fighting ground.

"The Conversation" for Understanding Endurance in Faith

God doesn't give us all the details about where we are going, because He will use not only the destination but the journey to teach us how to hear His voice in the fight. This journey of faith is tied to our belief in God's character, His power, His faithfulness, and His sovereignty. I had my own journey and battlefield experience that rewired my emotional memories and perspective of God from a rule-based, ritual experience to a relational safety net.

In creating my company, Living Strong Consulting, I have experienced many times when I had no idea what God was doing. I clung to the opportunity to play small and keep things manageable and within my control, but the inner desire and whispers from my God kept pulling me to want more and learn to let go and trust His character—even when I could not see the next step or the solution to the problem in front of me, in the natural realm. I had to learn to trust that He is always still working in the spiritual realm to create supernatural outcomes that continue to blow my mind and that train my eye to see him in the struggle and the victory.

Can I suggest to you that God may be using your test to train your ear to hear Him under pressure?

This experience with God is not about knowing where you are going. He is already ahead of you and committed to fulfilling the promises mapped out for you. God has offered us more than 8,000 promises in the Bible that are within our reach if we would just step out and grab them. But that requires us to trust him. God has promised to meet our every need, but that promise comes with the condition that we must trust Him. And the more we trust Him, the more He is able to meet our needs.

So how can we learn to trust Him more?

How can we learn to have greater faith?

The process of building faith I'm describing is not a "grueling, hold-on-for-dear-life, white-knuckle-grip survival" faith, but a strength process of *endurance* with God that will refuel you each step of the way.

ENDURANCE: the act, quality, or power of withstanding hardship or stress; continuing under resistance or adversity; the ability to hold up under pressure

Why would God place this word, *endurance,* so deeply in my heart that every morning it pulls me to pen and paper to write? Maybe because learning the lesson of finishing strong was not just about getting *through* the race but more about *how* I ran the race of faith.

I have been a runner for years. It is my stress reliever and my regulator for mental processing. Each morning, I lace up my shoes and go on a journey for gaining clarity about what it means to endure physically, spiritually, mentally, and emotionally. My goal, my hope, my prayer is that on this journey with God, I will stretch and strengthen my muscles for a life lived more abundantly by not avoiding the inevitable pains and barriers in life but by exercising the inner strength and power seated deep in me (and in you) to run this race, whether it is to keep pace at work, leap hurdles in our finances, overcome obstacles in relationships, burn out a broken thought life, or build the endurance for a physical road race. The goal is to learn the strategies and tools embedded in this powerful word *endurance* that are offered through His promises.

I wish I could say that I have learned these lessons well or have a box of tools gained from only successful races all run well. No, that's not my story. But I can share the well-worn lessons of holding on when I thought I couldn't, taking another step when I thought my knees would surely buckle, and pressing forward with only enough light to see the path one step at a time. These are lessons of endurance taught by a Father who brought hope every morning, who caught each tear that I shed, and who has given me a sense of security that reaches beyond my understanding.

In this race of faith, we have the opportunity to unpack and apply endurance from the training plan of the Master Trainer, who is the author and finisher of our life, Jesus Christ. Whether you are actually training for a season of physical running, like me, or training for a day filled with hurdles, the principles of endurance are the same. Each of us is on our own raceway, a path of purpose, destiny, and calling with very real obstacles in our way to fulfillment and the finish line. What I have learned while writing this book, training for a marathon, and just living life is that endurance is required for all of it.

Ready? Let's go run your race of endurance.

Go to the Fearless Conversations with a Limitless God Video Companion at https://gumroad.com/livingstrongllc#. (Enter the discount code m88hm52 to access the video content for free.) Then watch our "Iron Sharpens Iron" Fearless Conversations video. Listen as these women share their personal stories of pain, victory, and revelation, and then answer the following questions. What is God revealing to you about your race of endurance and faith?

What test is God using in your life right now to build your muscle of faith?

_____

_____

_____

What tricks or schemes of the enemy do we need to become aware of that are used against us as weights in this race of endurance and faith?

_____

_____

_____

What triggers are repeating themselves and hindering your walk of faith?

_____

_____

_____

How could you use your painful experience(s) to bring purpose in reaching others?

_____

_____

_____

What life lessons can be used to help you understand your faith and increase your trust in the sovereignty of God?

_____

_____

_____

_____

_____

Take Action and Run Your Race

"Faith is like a muscle. The more you use it, the more powerful it becomes."
—Anonymous

I hate burpees! LOL. Whenever the trainer says, "Okay, it's time for our favorite. Let's knock these burpees out," I think, *Whose favorite are these!?*

But in the back of my mind, I know that they are the most effective full-body exercise that builds multiple muscle groups all at once. Ugh! In any effective training plan, the goal is to pull together exercises that build strength and endurance, which results in some painful recovery days. Still, I know the pain has a purpose. My plan is clear and set with intention: Finish the race strong!

In the same way, our loving and faithful God has set our course for a victorious finish. Some of the training plans for the race we run for Him may have steep mountains, downhill sprints with the wind to our back, or grueling strength sets where we think we just can't lift anymore.

The truth is that if instead of getting angry about the training plan, we shift our focus to the pending victory that is built into the plan—our endurance, our power, our focus, our stamina—we will ignite the purpose embedded in the plan, which rests in the palm of the hand of a God who faithfully orchestrates abundance for every runner He entrusts us with a race mapped out for victory. We will be able to finish strong and hear "Well done."

As I approach the challenges of each step of the running course, the office later today, the bumps in relationships, or the hurdles of negative self-talk, I have set my mind on the eternal prize (1 Corinthians 9:24–25) that Christ has for me. Fear, doubt, insecurities, self-imposed limitations, and limiting mindsets have been put on notice and removed from my wellness plan—mind, body, and spirit. I believe that a shift in my perspective—to find value in my story, to know that I am more than my past and that He has been equipping me for such a time as this—is the first step to the starting line for a day of abundance.

Tweak your perspective and ask yourself, "What do I bring to the starting line today? How will I use it to bring glory to God and abundance to my life?"

I tried on my daughter's weighted vest yesterday. She is a college athlete and has been training for collegiate-level sports since she was 12 years old. In researching the benefits of wearing a weighted vest to train, I discovered that wearing a weighted vest during training sessions increases strength and endurance for race day. The more weight used, the more the muscles have to adapt, which builds strength and muscular endurance. Research studies have shown that people who train with a weighted vest run farther, longer, and faster than their counterparts on race day. So, although wearing the weight during the training season is uncomfortable, places pressure on the runner, and makes the training period grueling ...

On race day, the purpose for the weight becomes clear.

On race day, the runner can physically, emotionally, and mentally feel the purpose of the previous weighted trial.

On race day, when there is a strength and endurance that pushes the runners past everything in their paths with a newly developed lung capacity that allows them to run longer, faster, and higher, purpose is revealed.

Are there trials, pressures, or burdens that you feel the weight of? Recognize that training has a purpose; it is for a season. Where you are today is no accident. Our Master Trainer is more concerned with your potential than with your comfort. God is using this training season to shape and prepare you for "Race Day": when the weight has been lifted; when your strength, endurance, stamina, and speed are fully revealed; and when you are at the finish line in the place you were destined to be.

Run. Soar. Be Free.

The Lord will work out his plans for my life, for your faithful love, O Lord, endures forever. Don't abandon me, for you made me.—**Psalm 138:8**

Begin to create an action plan that will challenge your mindset, your heart condition, your physical wealth, and your spiritual conditioning for the course laid out before you. Tackle the morning, replacing repeated patterns of doubt, fatigue, worry, and discouragement with a brilliant starter routine filled with opportunity. Fresh beginnings fuel courageous finishes. How you start your day will set the tone for how effectively you make an impact during the rest of your day.

Greatness and abundance are born when you are drawn to a goal and purpose that is incomprehensible—one that doesn't make sense! Your purpose is wrapped up in the boldness of "why you must make the change *now*." When you give intentional focus to the answer of that question and live a daily practice of moving in purpose on purpose, you begin to see the manifestation of a life that exceeds even your own thoughts, dreams, and desires. This process begins by starving your distractions and feeding your focus at the start of your day. Each morning, take 30 minutes to locate and study a resource (article, podcast, audiobook, YouTube clip, book chapter, etc.) that will teach you something new and move you closer to your changes in behavior, mindset, emotional strength, or physical endurance. Just 30 minutes each morning of training in a new skill, area of expertise, or way of thinking will grow you and your dreams for abundant living. Form a new habit. For the next seven days, write the title of the resource you used on the lines next.

Day 1 _____

Day 2 _____

Day 3 _____

Day 4 _____

Day 5 _____

Day 6 _____

Day 7 _____

Check out our Fearless Calendar in our eStore for visual daily planning of how to break broken patterns and live life to the fullest ... and running over ☺! https://gumroad.com/livingstrongllc#

Reflect on Your Growth

Take some time for focused reflection and intentional celebration. Review your journal or notes from this chapter. What are your top three takeaways from this experience?

_____

_____

_____

Why did those things stand out to you?

_____

_____

_____

    Mind. Body. Soul. Connection: Now let's restore some mental pathways through the therapeutic activity of coloring. Take this time to connect worship, prayer, music, and stillness while you focus on the creative act of coloring. Coloring has been found to reduce anxiety, increase focus, build awareness, and provide clarity. When you take the time to calm your mind, your brain enters a relaxed state by focusing on the present and blocking out the nonstop thinking we all experience. As a result, you reach a place of calm that relieves your brain from the daily stresses of life and allows you to continue to refresh and restore. So find your favorite worship song and a quiet place to sit, and let's start coloring.

DEUTERONOMY 31:6 (NIV) *"Be strong and courageous. Do not be afraid or terrified because of them, for the LORD your God goes with you; he will never leave you nor forsake you."*

Stepping into Peace

Basement: Traveling through the Valley

THE FIRST STEP IN CONQUERING the battlefield of the mind is to recognize when you are entering into the battle. Often, to get to the good places in our journey, we must travel through the bad. But thankfully, we are never traveling alone. The Lord has gifts, plans, and treasures for each of us, but in our travels they are often on the other side of our comfort zone. On the surface, our preferred comfort level would be to understand all that must be done to receive all there is to offer within our reach, but we can find a gift in the place of uncertainty and discomfort. It's in those moments of uncertainty that He challenges us, teaches us, reminds us, and holds us to the understanding of "not my will, but His." His grace is sufficient. There's no need for faith and grace if we know how to do everything ourselves, have all the answers, and control all the outcomes—and continue to live small within the boundaries of our certain control. He is a loving God and provider—a place of safety, peace, and help. We can only learn to trust His character in situations where we are uncomfortable, and that only happens when we step out.

For example, when I entered into a project that I had been assigned and felt inadequate for, I heard myself say, *"I want you to use me, Lord, in such an awe-inspiring way that I am knocked to my knees by your love and provision."* But what I am learning is that this cannot happen if the journey to the blessing always makes sense and is comfortable. Then there would be no surprise, wonder, or confirmation of His providing character. To know His character is at the heart of my goal.

The origin of the word *comfort* in Latin is *confortare*, which means "to strengthen much." Lord, I accept Your challenge to gain a deeper understanding that true comfort in You does not mean avoiding pain, but that you will come into my every day to carry my pain and help me experience much strength with you. Even in the valley moments of my life.

PSALM 23:4 *Yes, though I walk through the valley of the shadow of death, I will fear no evil; For You are with me; Your rod and Your staff, they comfort me.*

It is in those valley moments that I learn the character of God because I experience His strength, stability, and girding when I feel threatened by the shadow, but I also realize there cannot be a shadow if there isn't light as well. Even in those dark valley moments, the light of our God is present. He's there! My comfort comes with the strength and stability of the Shepherd's rod and staff. The rod represents protection from outward dangers, and the staff represents correction and boundaries when I am wandering. Psalm 23:4 reminds us of two types of enemies that show up in our fight in the valley in the presence of our Shepherd. For the external fight that I need protection from, our Shepherd's rod becomes a safeguard when threat enters my life. The second enemy is the enemy in me. The staff is used for those times when my internal battle in my mind, soul, and spirit begins to create distraction and confusion. He stays with me even when I stray from Him. The staff is designed as a tool with a big hook on the end. It is used to hook onto wandering sheep. I remember a time when, although I had been beaten up by the offenses and hurts of an external enemy, it was the internal wounds that I battled with as I tried to pull away from God. The emotions of anger, bitterness, fear, and frustration had a field day in my mind and distorted my perspective of God based on my perception of man. But no matter how hard I tried to run from Him, his staff encircled me in safety. His patience offered a mercy and grace that looped me in and gave me peace beyond my understanding—so much so that reflecting on His character and consistency in those times brings me safety and security in my battles now.

Awareness: Shoes of Peace

One of the top things the enemy goes after in a battle is our peace, because if he can steal our peace, he robs from our relationships, our

mental focus, our active engagement in our gifts, and the steps of our calling. Preparation for those steps can be impacted by the type of shoes we walk in.

If you were a pair of shoes, what shoe would you be? And why?

_____

_____

_____

_____

_____

EPHESIANS 6:13–18 (MSG) *Be prepared. You're up against far more than you can handle on your own. Take all the help you can get, every weapon God has issued, so that when it's all over but the shouting, you'll still be on your feet. Truth, righteousness, peace, faith, and salvation are more than words. Learn how to apply them. You'll need them throughout your life. God's Word is an indispensable weapon. In the same way, prayer is essential in this ongoing warfare. Pray hard and long. Pray for your brothers and sisters. Keep your eyes open. Keep each other's spirits up so that no one falls behind or drops out.*

Paul tells us in the passage above that the battle is fierce. We will come up against more than we can handle all alone. We need to acknowledge that we must use every weapon God has offered so that we are still standing on our feet when the dust settles. He goes on to list the weapons God offers as parts of armor for the battle: truth, righteousness, peace, faith, and salvation. However, he wants to also make sure we understand that these are more than just words. The New Living Translation (NLT) interpretation of Ephesians 6:14–15 illuminates the instruction of standing and the armor needed to be able to keep our grounding.

EPHESIANS 6:14–15 (NLT) *Stand your ground, putting on the belt of truth and the body armor of God's righteousness. **For shoes, put on the peace that comes from the Good News so that you will be fully prepared.***

To represent the source of protection for our healthy relationships, settled mind, execution of our gifts, and preparation in our calling, he uses the image of shoes.

How do you define the importance of peace in your life and your calling?

_____

_____

_____

_____

The shoe Paul uses to represent peace would have been familiar to readers during that time, because the shoes used in battle were a Roman caligae. They were designed from three leather layers: an outsole, the middle boot, and an insole. Iron hobnails were hammered into the soles to provide the caligae with reinforcement and traction, and they were also an effective weapon against a fallen enemy. Thinking about the value of shoes, why would Paul attach the image of shoes to something Satan comes after so fiercely as our peace?

Write down how the lack of peace can impact your life.

_____

_____

_____

_____

This makes me think of our conversation about the Israelites at the Red Sea and their enemy, pharaoh and his chariots, running them down. God's battle plan was not to equip them with power and strength physically to overtake pharaoh's army but to strengthen them mentally by shifting their mental state by instructing them to not fear, stand firm, and watch God provide their salvation. The focus was not on the ability to run or fight but to stand firm and get grounded emotionally, physically, mentally, and spiritually. In a very similar way, the caligae was not designed for a quick escape, but for standing sure-footedly in battle and attacking the enemy under your feet. **Romans 16:20 (NLT)** *"The God of peace will soon crush Satan under your feet. May the grace of our Lord Jesus be with you."* The lesson to be taught in these moments is far deeper than "just escape." He wants us to dig in the hobnails of faith and be sure-footed with peace in the grounding we get from recognizing His presence and seeing His strength as God.

What do those hobnails represent as we stand firm in life?

_____

_____

_____

_____

Hobnails on caligae provide the warrior with a depth of stance, traction when the terrain gets slippery, stability in turbulent storms, and counterattack when the enemy is down. We can't avoid rocky roads, tough storms, or changing terrain as we go to new heights in life, but it's actually the tests of the rocky roads that will reassure us that we have the right shoes on when it is time to come out of the valley. What I have discovered, though, is that if you have not built your stamina to endure the valley experience, you will never survive the grueling demands of a mountaintop experience.

Understanding: Surviving Elevated Places

So often I hear people say things like …
 "If I could just get to the next level …"
 "If I could just rise above this situation …"

"I can't wait to get to the top ..."

"When I make it out of this valley experience to the top of my game, ..."

Each of these statements makes it sound like getting to the top of a scenario, situation, problem, position, opportunity, or status is an *arrival*! You made it ... now rest!

Well, I have run the peaks of elevated places, and after coming out of the valley, there is no easy terrain at the top. Elevated places are actually where the work begins. If you aren't ready and haven't trained for the opportunity, you will *lose it* on the slopes, rocky surface, unpredictable obstacles, and uncertainty of uneven terrain on the mountaintop! Although the valley has a specific role, you have not been *chosen* to stay there. You have not been *chosen* for the valley. I can hear you say, "If I wasn't chosen for the valley, why should I have to go through it at all?"

Our youngest daughter is 18 years old now, but her father started training her as an athlete by having her wear a weighted vest during training sessions when she was 12 years old.

One afternoon, we were shopping for her things to prepare for college, and she asked, "Did you and Dad have any idea that I would be going to college as an athlete when I was little?" The question made me stop dead in my tracks. I paused, smiled, and told her, "You were hours old in the hospital, and your father took you from my arms and carried you to the window of the hospital to show you the elite track and field of the university next door to the hospital. He whispered in your ear, 'You will run on fields like that one day.'" Did we ever think? Your father spoke your destiny from your beginning.

Did we ever think? Yes, your father had plans for you from the start; you just had to want them too and work it out!

What also struck me was that she asked her question about the current elevated place she was in like it *just happened.* Like the years of running in that weighted vest, lifting weights, practicing, and training didn't happen. I realized in that moment that she had integrated the training into her calling and was not stuck by, stuck in, bitter over, or embarrassed by anything she had to go through in the training season to get to this elevated point. Her father had put her through a rigorous training plan that cost her time, energy, effort, tears, sweat, and courage because he was more invested in the process than just the end product, because he had already spoken that victory over her life! Now, she just had to work it out. She went through it to have the endurance and strength to remain in the elevated places He had plans for her.

1 PETER 5:10 (NKJV) *But may the God of all grace, who called us to His eternal glory by Christ Jesus, **after you have suffered a while, perfect, establish, strengthen, and settle you.***

Go to the Fearless Conversations with a Limitless God Video Companion at https://gumroad.com/livingstrongllc#. (Enter the discount code m88hm52 to access the video content for free.) Then watch our "Iron Sharpens Iron" Fearless Conversations video.

Listen as these women share their personal stories of pain, victory, and revelation, and then answer the following questions. What is God revealing to you about establishing sure footing in the process of gaining more peace in your life?

How does a valley struggle with safety and trust directly impact our inner sense of peace—emotionally, physically, mentally, relationally, and spiritually?

_____

_____

_____

_____

What do we need to be aware of about the dimensions of safety (being safe with self, others, and our God)?

_____

_____

_____

_____

_____

How can telling our story turn a valley experience into a message of peace, acceptance, and freedom?

_____

_____

_____

_____

_____

What are some action steps for establishing peace in our daily walk with God and others?

_____

_____

_____

_____

_____

What life lessons have you learned about using trust, safety, and peace to fortify your walk as a woman of God through different types of life's terrain?

_____

_____

_____

_____

_____

Training Happens in the Valley so that Purpose Is Revealed in Elevated Places

What does it mean to be chosen?

_____

_____

_____

_____

_____

JOHN 15:16 (NKJV) *You did not choose Me, but I chose you and appointed you that you should go and bear fruit, and that your fruit should remain, that whatever you ask the Father in My name He may give you.*

There's a responsibility that comes with being chosen and placed in elevated places. When I mention elevated places, I am talking not only about platforms or titles. Elevated places can be leading as a woman of God at the dinner table with your family; elevating the awareness in a meeting where integrity is missing; showing up in an authentic way every time you enter the classroom, boardroom, or prayer closet; being obedient in forgiving that person God has been telling you to release from bitterness; and loving when it is hard. Elevation is not about the position or platform you are on but the obedience of your heart and mind to the assignment you are given. It's positioning your walk in peace in such a way that the character traits required for your calling are utilized to produce fruit that will remain beyond you.

In Greek, "called" is *kletos*, which means "accepting the benefits of salvation as an act of God." "Chosen" in Greek is *eklektos*, which means "to be selected." So after accepting the calling, we are required to live a life as a chosen and selected woman of God. Further, the called and chosen are required to be faithful. In Greek, "faithful" is *pistos*, which means "to be trusted, reliable, active, believing." The called and chosen can be trusted and relied on to be obedient to what they have been called to do. Many are called, but few are chosen! Few are prepared to walk out the life they have been chosen for. Since God:

Created me
Chose me
Redeemed me
Saved me
Changed me
Transformed me
Gave me a new life
Made me a new creature

He has designated me with a task for the elevated life that I must live. The fruit of my life is for those around me, behind me, and in front of me. What I have gone through is not about me. It's about my fruit.

Your elevation has to happen. Are you willing to complete the training process for it?

EPHESIANS 4:1–7 (ESV) *I therefore, a prisoner for the Lord, urge you to walk in a manner worthy of the calling to which you have been called, with all humility and gentleness, with patience, bearing with one another in love, eager to maintain the unity of the Spirit in the bond of peace. There is one body and one Spirit—just as you were called to the one hope that belongs to your call—one Lord, one faith, one baptism, one God and Father of all, who is over all and through all and in all. But grace was given to each one of us according to the measure of Christ's gift.*

Thinking about those hobnails, that preparation to walk in peace to fulfill our calling connects to the depth of stance that comes from our rootedness in the Word of God. The process of gaining sure footing provides us with two types of peace when walking in our calling:

Peace with God
Peace of God

Peace with God fills our heart with the natural yearning of a need for peace. Our very souls yearn for the peace offered with God, and He pulls us to Him. The gift He offers and leaves with us is His peace. Peace is so vitally important to our mind, body, and spirit that in John 14:27 (ESV) he packages this gift as a declaration and instruction. The peace He offers does not look like what the world offers but is one that will offer the grounding needed to stand firm in our calling in the middle of the world's distractions without adopting the traits of the world wrapped in fear, worry, stress, and anxiousness. Out of our relationship with Him, that peace with God allows us to display the fruit of the Peace of God in elevated places. And as one who is chosen, the peace of God helps us work in unity with others and in peace for God. With the peace He offers, we are able to access humility, gentleness, patience, love, and unity.

But we have a very real enemy who is after this active peace in us. Satan is strategic, intentional, and organized with his assault, so we must be the same way when creating our battle plan for walking, maintaining, and living a life of peace.

How can we access this peace, so that it becomes integrated into our mind, body, and spirit on a daily basis? Well, it goes back to our earlier Scripture, Ephesians 6:13–18 (MSG), and the armor we wear for the battle. There are pieces of armor that are worn or put on, but there is one weapon that is essential and is actively set in motion against our enemy. It also works for our fellow warriors, and it seals this process of peace.

EPHESIANS 6:13–18 (MSG) *Be prepared. You're up against far more than you can handle on your own. Take all the help you can get, every weapon God has issued, so that when it's all over but the shouting, you'll still be on your feet. Truth, righteousness, peace, faith, and salvation are more than words. Learn how to apply them. You'll need them throughout your life. God's Word is an indispensable* weapon. *In the same way, prayer is essential in this ongoing warfare. Pray hard and long. Pray for your brothers and sisters. Keep your eyes open. Keep each other's spirits up so that no one falls behind or drops out.*

Your greatest weapon against Satan's attacks is your targeted assault from your knees in prayer. It ignites God's faithfulness into action for your protection and also for the protection of every name on your battle plan list. I want you to think about not just *what* armor the soldiers wore, but *how* the soldiers went into battle. No soldier goes into battle alone. You are not alone, and as a Prayer Warrior, you also cover each member battling with you.

For the next 30 days, schedule a time of prayer as you would any other appointment on your calendar. Create a Prayer Calendar and label each date box with the name of family, friends, and colleagues you will go into battle for with an intentional 30-day assault on the enemy covered by our Father's faithfulness for established victory.

1	2	3	4	5
6	7	8	9	10
11	12	13	14	15
16	17	18	19	20
21	22	23	24	25
26	27	28	29	30

Another assault weapon that establishes our footing and increases our peace is replacing worry, fear, anxiety, and regret with **prayer, praise,** and **worship.**

PHILIPPIANS 4:6–7 (MSG) *Don't fret or worry. Instead of worrying, pray. Let petitions and praises shape your worries into prayers, letting God know your concerns. Before you know it, a sense of God's wholeness, everything coming together for good, will come and settle you down. It's wonderful what happens when Christ displaces worry at the center of your life.*

"When fear knocks, let faith answer the door." —Robin Roberts

Write your prayer requests here. For every thought that robs you of peace, write a prayer in response with your faith.

_____

_____

_____

_____

Check out our Fearless Calendar in our eStore for visual daily prayers of how to break broken patterns and live life to the fullest ... and running over! https://gumroad.com/livingstrongllc#

Rest in Reflection: What Has God Revealed to You?

How can your responses and reactions change in situations with a greater assurance of peace?

_____

_____

_____

Take some time for focused reflection and intentional celebration. Review your journal or notes from this chapter. What are your top three takeaways from this experience?

_____

_____

_____

Why did those things stand out to you?

_____

_____

_____

_____

Mind. Body. Soul. Connection: Now let's restore some mental pathways through the therapeutic activity of coloring. Take this time to connect worship, prayer, music, and stillness while you focus on the creative act of coloring. Coloring has been found to reduce anxiety, increase focus, build awareness, and provide clarity. When you take the time to calm your mind, your brain enters a relaxed state by focusing on the present and blocking out the nonstop thinking we all experience. As a result, you reach a place of calm that relieves your brain from the daily stresses of life and allows you to continue to refresh and restore. So find your favorite worship song and a quiet place to sit, and let's start coloring.

ISAIAH 26:3 *You will keep in perfect peace those whose minds are steadfast, because they trust in you.*

Power and Purpose Are a Passion, Not a Platform

Basement: Making the Decision

She would have been at the back of the space. Her *issues* were too many to allow her to be *in* the space with others. But there was something *in* her that day that screamed louder than her pain. It was the call of her purpose!

Her issues were so profound that they consumed her name; she is known only as the Woman With The Issue of Blood. Dictionary.com defines "identity" as *"who someone is, the qualities or beliefs that make a particular person or group different from others."* It's that thing that sets us apart from the crowd. For the woman in Luke 8:43, this distinction was her issues.

LUKE 8:43 (MSG) *In the crowd that day there was a woman who for 12 years had been afflicted with hemorrhages. She had spent every penny she had on doctors, but not one had been able to help her.*

But is she so different from any of us? No, we may not be physically bleeding, but are we hemorrhaging the loss of parts of who we are— our value, identity, passion, focus, strength? Are you losing what makes you distinctly different? Not the false identity of the "to do" list, tasks, or accolades you have acquired, but the unique essence of the God-created you that shifts the atmosphere every time you enter a room? So often, I have held the hands of women who have lost sight of the distinctions of this truth. I, myself, got so lost in the issues surrounding me, consuming me, and pulling me that I struggled to find any image of a "fearfully made" me in the mirror. My ability and achievement, or lack thereof, became *my definition of me.* How often can we lose sight of the fact that we are not what we do or what has happened to us? Getting clear about this truth is at the core of leading your life on purpose and tapping into the power of God to use you in the unique identity created only for you.

Finding the strength, fortitude, and boldness to look each day in the face on purpose requires us to lead in our positions, tasks, and roles and also in our lives with the intention of transformation. It requires creating a shift in our mindset from "doing" to "being," which will take us on a journey in which we discover the purpose, passion, priority, and promise of God within us. With clarity about each of these, even when the platform is shaky or life isn't looking like what we thought it should, our identity is rooted in something deeper than our circumstances. But shifting from task building to identity building requires removing the mask and making a decision.

Let's explore how this woman "with issues" allows her journey of trust to lead her to being healed on purpose for her purposed destiny, and how it all started with making a decision. Matthew tells the same story but lets us see even more detail about what shifted with this woman with issues that made that different from any other day.

MATTHEW 9:20–21 *Then a woman who had suffered from a hemorrhage for 12 years came up behind Him and touched the [tassel] fringe of His outer robe;* **for she had been saying to herself, "If I only touch His outer robe, I will be healed."**

What does the word *breakthrough* mean? Write your definition here:

_____

_____

_____

_____

_____

One definition of *breakthrough* is "*a moment in time when there is an opening.*" Let's unpack how a woman opens her thought life and intentionally walks out of her mess into her breakthrough with her mindset on being healed on purpose.

But, let's be honest, at the start of this passage, this woman felt anything but *"open"* after more than 12 years of accumulated stress. She had a medical issue with her blood, but was that her only issue? With this one issue came several others: She was physically weak, financially weak, socially weak and isolated, and emotionally weak.

Have you ever noticed that we can start off holding on to one issue and then it grows into multiple issues?

I can hear and see her looking at her life and saying, "It's not supposed to be like this." The image of who she felt she was meant to be as a woman was clashing with the reality of how her issues were defining her. The building stress of her issues created a breaking weight and a load to her life, and on that morning she decided to shift out from under them.

Thinking about women today, I know that some of us can relate to how the allostatic load, or overload of life, can press us down emotionally, physically, and mentally. In 1993, the term *allostatic load* was coined by researchers Bruce S. McEwen and Elliot Stellar. Allostatic load refers to the long-term effects of continued exposure to chronic stress on the body, the "wear and tear" that takes a toll on our body systems and our ability to mentally see beyond our current condition.

Science shows us that seeking a breakthrough from compounded stress is about our mental state as well as our physical state. It's not just the occasional maladaptive behavior that hinders us. It's the chronic cycle of broken habits that creates an unbearable weight on our being, as we try to adapt over and over to this shifting weight in life. Chronic worry, high-pressure positions, toxic relationships, prolonged isolation, financial difficulties, poor habits, and self-defeating thoughts create a load on our minds and bodies that hinders us from functioning, keeping us trapped in health problems and even shortening our life expectancy.

We can begin to break through this load on our life by increasing our awareness of how this state is impacting our lives and making a clear decision that *Christ has set us free to live a free life. So take your stand! Never again let anyone put a harness of slavery on you.* (Galatians 5:1) (MSG) This is an intentional act of getting clear about what we are entitled to—that our inheritance is for a life designed and destined by a God offering freedom.

That's the mind space I can see this *Woman with the issue of blood* waking up to on this day. Matthew 9:21 (NKJV) states, *For she said within herself, "If I may but touch his garment, I shall be made whole."* She talked to herself at the start to set her priority for healing. In the Greek, the phrase *"For she said within herself"* describes not a passing statement but a repeated statement. Can you see her moving through the house that morning as she said over and over again to herself, *"If I may but touch his garment, I shall be made whole"*? She said it aloud as she reached for her dress, which was likely worn from years of wear because she had no financial way to replace it. She said it as she reached for her sandals, which were tattered and torn from the many uneventful trips to physicians and specialists who provided her with no help for her issues. She said it to herself as she washed her face, which was tired from years of disappointment. With each release of the words, she felt more determined and clearer. She continued to repeat that statement to herself with each block she walked as she headed through the crowd. Can you hear how it changed in tone with each step, building with momentum and determination as the truth of the words began to resonate in her soul? The load she had accumulated and carried for 12 years was not hers to carry. She would pick it up one last time, only to deliver it to the feet of the Christ she had heard so much about and knew in the depths of her core was the source for her healing. She set the priority that she would be made whole by Christ today!

That's the power of breakthrough for this woman. No, she had not yet been physically healed, but she was mentally open to everything that she knew she was entitled to and getting clear that she would not carry this load another day. This created the break that made her bold enough to leave isolation and enter the populated place where her Christ stood. The power of her breakthrough started with her priority to make a decision.

What are you willing to decide today?

_____

_____

_____

What load will you put down today?

_____

_____

_____

What level of freedom do you want to access today?

_____

_____

_____

What would a breakthrough look like for you today?

_____

_____

_____

Awareness: Taking Steps of Humility for Healing

LUKE 8:43–45 (MSG) *In the crowd that day there was a woman who for 12 years had been afflicted with hemorrhages. She had spent every penny she had on doctors, but not one had been able to help her. **She slipped in from behind and touched the edge of Jesus' robe. At that very moment her hemorrhaging stopped.** Jesus said, "Who touched me?"*

A woman who was courageous enough to have a priority of healing took a position of humility to gain the attention of Jesus and access His power.

To touch the edge (hem) of Jesus's robe, what position would she have to take? Being low, unnoticed, or out of the way was probably a usual position for her. During that time, because of her medical issue with her blood, she would have been viewed as unclean. This would leave her isolated and ostracized. How ironic it is that surviving our past hurts can sometimes give us approaches to life that can be leveraged in painful moments to set us up for victorious finishes. In the process of pressing her way to the hem of Jesus, she turned her past experience of moving through crowds in lowness and shame inside out to a determined pursuit of humility by positioning herself to be low enough to reach His feet. It would not be those clawing and pushing and pressing for attention who stood up high who made Jesus stop. It was a woman not caught up in what she felt entitled to in the flesh but humbled by her press for the gift offered by Jesus's very presence at His feet.

And then it happens …

LUKE 8:45–46 (MSG) *Jesus said, "Who touched me?" When no one stepped forward, Peter said, "But Master, we've got crowds of people on our hands. Dozens have touched you." Jesus insisted, "Someone touched me. I felt power discharging from me."*

Peter's statement highlights a sobering fact that you can be in and around the crowd and still not tap into His power. If you just show up, you can still be left out. It is not that you *showed up* for the Bible study, church service, women's conference, or prayer meeting. Just showing up is not enough. There were throngs of people in that crowd pressing against Jesus and creating activity, noise, and distraction for Jesus, but only one tapped into the power of Jesus. This scene challenges us to become aware of how we are positioning our hearts when we enter the presence of Jesus. This woman may have needed to enter the space physically low, but it was the elevated position of her heart to be passionate about who she was seeking and the increased clarity of her mental state that positioned her for a real encounter with Him.

And He stopped and asked, "Who touched me?"

Why would an all-knowing God ask, "Who touched me?" Understand that it was not because He didn't know. He knew who she was and where she was, but it was now time for her to take a new position, no longer behind the crowd, but in front of the crowd. Her perspective about herself had shifted at home when she left making that bold declaration for change in order to pursue the Christ, but it was now time for everyone else who had looked past her, looked over her, and moved away from her to know of her change in position as well. It was time to reveal her to everyone in order that her purpose behind her pain would become her platform for her testimony.

LUKE 8:46–47 (MSG) *When no one stepped forward, Peter said, "But Master, we've got crowds of people on our hands. Dozens have touched you." Jesus insisted, "Someone touched me. I felt power discharging from me." When the woman realized that she couldn't remain hidden, she knelt trembling before him. In front of all the people, she blurted out her story—why she touched him and how at that same moment she was healed.*

There is purpose in "your issue" and in "that pain" that can be a testimony to others. God will use everything in your life to season the lives of others. When I speak with groups of women, I use a visual of two pans. I ask the *real* cooks in the audience, "Which pan would you reach for if you *really* wanted to cook?" The veteran cooks immediately point to the worn, beaten-up, scratched-up cast-iron pan—almost every time. Why on Earth would they immediately pick a pan that has clearly seen better days and has weathered the storms of some long, heated moments over a shiny frying pan that is clearly fresh and polished? Inevitably, someone always says to me, "Because it's *seasoned*." Yes, exactly! That cast-iron pan has been through some

things in life, and it has gotten scraped and scuffed in the process. But in the folds of those scuffs, the seasoning that has been applied in each fiery moment has been baked into the pan's very essence, and now it has value for being used. We are facing dying, hurting, and lost times. People who have bought into the shiny, polished version of "showing up" at pristine religious events have been left empty with little substance offered. It is not so much about where you come from, what your hang-up might be, or even the load you are carrying. It is about the authentic heart of your worship that has been seasoned with experiences of Faith. He will take and use that for His glory. If we will humble ourselves and be willing to just show up with an authentic heart, honest and true, He will receive us and turn that heart of worship into a message that saves lives.

And do you know what happened next? When she was vulnerable with Him and trusted Him with her issue? She laid it before him and in front of everyone. She traded her hurt for a new relationship with Christ. Their relationship changed. Until this point in the story, she had been named for her issue, identified by her issue, and categorized by her issue, but now her heart was revealed, and their relationship changed. He called her "daughter"!

LUKE 8:47–48 (MSG) *When the woman realized that she couldn't remain hidden, she knelt trembling before him. In front of all the people, she blurted out her story—why she touched him and how at that same moment she was healed. Jesus said, "Daughter, you took a risk trusting me, and now you're healed and whole. Live well, live blessed!"*

We all have come with issues. We can choose to lay them at the feet of Jesus or continue to hold on to them. I know being vulnerable and open can be scary, but will you take the risk and trust Him? Allow Him to do work in you as His daughter.

Understanding: The Process Is More Important Than Your Destination

LUKE 8:48 (MSG) *Jesus said, "Daughter, you took a risk trusting me, and now you're healed and whole. Live well, live blessed!"*

Christ gives this woman the charge to "live well, live blessed!" What does it mean to you to live well?

_____

_____

_____

_____

_____

So often living well or blessed can look like perfection for women. But He does not call us to perfection, but to excellence in Him. How would you define the word *excellence*? What if we viewed excellence not through the perspective of our culture—"looking for perfection"—but from God's perspective—"looking for passion"? Actually, perfection is often just another hiding place for our fear of not being enough. Perfectionism provides a cloak over the fear of really being seen or known. We fear that if we are actually seen, it will be discovered that we don't measure up, we are not enough, or we just aren't valued. But this vivid picture in Scripture paints a very different image of what our Christ is seeking, which isn't perfection. Amongst all of the noise, the pushing, the chaos, He stops to speak to her and affirm her. He *sees* her. This gentle and loving conversation speaks to a woman far from perfect but full of passion.

As with this woman who came to Him just as she was, carrying the load of her life with her to His feet, He is not looking for women to show up in perfection. He wants passionate women living *on purpose* for Him. In His hands, God will use *every* experience, blunder, and broken place to continue to write your story, provide you with new chapters that exceed what you could ask or think, and confirm your purpose with exceeding grace. But in that journey of walking through and in your purpose, God is more interested in the process than the destination. He is more interested in your process or the shift in your decisions, your faith, and your endurance and fight.

Many of life's battles are won or lost in the mind. With every test, we stand at the crossroads of being bitter or better, broken or built up, victim or victor. This woman's story represents how we all can begin to break the cycle of toxic thoughts and shift life's load of circumstances that contradict God's promises of abundance in a life lived well. The average person has about 70,000 thoughts a day, and science is revealing more and more that patterns of toxic thoughts and toxic stress contribute to medical conditions including heart disease, asthma, diabetes, strokes, cancer, and skin problems. Renewing our mind is not just a childhood memory verse to be tucked away for safe keeping, but requires divine, commanded instruction for daily victorious living. The woman's shift started in her mind that morning when she decided to pursue Jesus and her healing. With so much connected to our thought life, it goes to reason that you are what you T.H.I.N.K. And with the instruction to capture any thought that is against our God and make it obedient (2 Corinthians 10:5), being intentional about processing our process becomes a life-saving practice. Using this acrostic poem for T.H.I.N.K., take some time to really think about your battle plan and shift your focus to the promises God has built into your experiences.

Tested by fire: How will you "choose" to respond to the stress and people in your life that are testing your faith?

_____

_____

_____

Healed for a purpose: How could you use your experiences to bring purpose in reaching others?

_____

_____

_____

Influence to others: Who is one person you think God put in your life for a reason or for a season? What is the reason? How can your influence play a role?

_____

_____

_____

No matter what faith: What is one goal you have for strengthening your relationship with God?

_____

_____

_____

Knowing you're enough: How can you use what you already have to bring glory to God? Just as you are …

_____

_____

_____

Go to the Fearless Conversations with a Limitless God Video Companion at https://gumroad.com/livingstrongllc#. (Enter the discount code m88hm52 to access the video content for free.) Then watch our "Iron Sharpens Iron" Fearless Conversations video. Listen as these women share their life lessons on accessing the power of God for a life well lived. Then reflect on your answers to the questions above. What is God revealing to you about living well and being blessed?

Take Action for Your Healing

Will you allow God to use everything in you to reach for your purpose—even if it requires vulnerability? _Jesus said, "Daughter, you **took a risk trusting me**, and now you're healed and whole. Live well, live blessed!"_ Christ acknowledged that in her vulnerable place, His daughter was taking a risk in trading her hurt for His healing. I mean, she had been disappointed time and time again, for 12 years, but something had shifted in her this time that ignited not just her natural knowing but her supernatural belief. To access the new places He will take us in our healing process requires us to take risks and to be vulnerable.

How do you define being vulnerable?

_____

_____

_____

_____

You see, being vulnerable is not weakness. It's an opportunity for us to access a deeper place of faith and submission for the creative energy of our God to take shape. When we take our hands off, loosening the grip of what we are familiar with and opening ourselves to His wondrous power, vulnerability becomes the platform for everything new in our lives. That's sometimes easier said than done. The familiar, even the dysfunctional familiar, can become comfortable. (It might be dysfunctional, but it's my dysfunction, and I know it far better than the mysteries of doing something new.) The Biblical passage leads us to understand that vulnerability is courageous as well. Can you hear the woman's heart beating as she takes on the glares from onlookers telling her that she was *too close to* Christ, or the initial horror in others' eyes that someone deemed unclean had reached for the Christ's robe? Even with her heart pounding, she didn't let the thoughts to go back and hide stop her. She reached anyway—not knowing what might happen, but filled with an unbridled faith of what *could* happen. She had to do something new. It was worth the risk!

In Him, we are new! What new thing, habit, or routine are you willing to embrace today? He did not just clean up the old thing. He is doing a completely new thing in each of us. How will you present this new state in an outward acknowledgment? It is already happening on the inside of you. That newness has been offered to you, not just for yourself, but for those who watch and enter your life. How can we deny them what God is doing inside of each of us? The old course of life is done. Christ offers us a new opportunity to walk boldly in who we are in Him. So let's shed the old mindset, take off the worn-out worries, and shake off the clinging old habits.

Create the setup for some new habits:

1. **Set your priority to follow Him.** Clean out Doubt/Fear and replace it with a clear decision of Faith.

- *You will keep in perfect peace those whose minds are steadfast, because they trust in you.* (Isaiah 26:3)
- *For God so loved the world that he gave his one and only Son, that whoever believes in him shall not perish but have eternal life.* (John 3:16)

2. **Set your position to pursue Him.** Clean out Pride and replace it with Humility.
   - *But he gives us more grace. That is why Scripture says: "God opposes the proud but gives grace to the humble."* (James 4:6)
   - *He guides the humble in what is right and teaches them His way.* (Psalm 25:9)

3. **Set your passion for excellence in Him.** Clean out Complaining and replace it with Praise.
   - *Do everything without complaining or arguing.* (Philippians 2:14)
   - *Through Jesus, therefore, let us continually offer to God a sacrifice of praise—the fruit of lips that confess his name. And do not forget to do good and to share with others, for with such sacrifices God is pleased.* (Hebrews 13:15–16)

4. **Set your eyes on the promises of God for your purpose.** Clean out Toxic Thoughts and replace them with Encouragement.
   - *Whatever is true, whatever is noble, whatever is right, whatever is pure, whatever is lovely, whatever is admirable—if anything is excellent or praiseworthy—think about such things.* (Philippians 4:8)
   - *But those who hope in the Lord will renew their strength. They will soar on wings like eagles; they will run and not grow weary, they will walk and not be faint.* (Isaiah 40:31)

In the next 24 hours, what do you need to do to access the renewal that God offers us?

_____

_____

_____

In the next 7 days …

_____

_____

_____

In the next 30 days ...

_____

_____

_____

_____

Check out our Fearless Calendar in our eStore for visual daily goal setting to break broken patterns and live life to the fullest ... and running over ☺! https://gumroad.com/livingstrongllc# ...

Reflect on Your Growth

Take some time for focused reflection and intentional celebration. Review your journal or notes from this chapter. What are your top three takeaways from this experience?

_____

_____

_____

Why did those things stand out to you?

_____

_____

_____

    Mind. Body. Soul. Connection: Now let's restore some mental pathways through the therapeutic activity of coloring. Take this time to connect worship, prayer, music, and stillness while you focus on the creative act of coloring. Coloring has been found to reduce anxiety, increase focus, build awareness, and provide clarity. When you take the time to calm your mind, your brain enters a relaxed state by focusing on the present and blocking out the nonstop thinking we all experience. As a result, you reach a place of calm that relieves your brain from the daily stresses of life and allows you to continue to refresh and restore. So find your favorite worship song and a quiet place to sit, and let's start coloring.

EPHESIANS 1:15–21 (NKJV) *Therefore I also, after I heard of your faith in the Lord Jesus and your love for all the saints, do not cease to give thanks for you, making mention of you in my prayers: that the God of our Lord Jesus Christ, the Father of glory, may give to you the spirit of wisdom and revelation in the knowledge of Him, the eyes of your understanding being enlightened; that you may know what is the hope of His calling, what are the riches of the glory of His inheritance in the saints, and what is the exceeding greatness of His power toward us who believe, according to the working of His mighty power which He worked in Christ when He raised Him from the dead and seated Him at His right hand in the heavenly places, far above all principality and power and might and dominion, and every name that is named, not only in this age but also in that which is to come.*

You Are Enough

Basement: You Are Not a Prisoner to Your Past

ESTHER 2:17 (NKJV) *The king loved Esther more than all the other women, and she obtained grace and favor in his sight more than all the virgins; so he set the royal crown upon her head and made her queen instead of Vashti.*

Do you know what the name *Esther* means? In the Persian dialect, it was a derivative of the goddess Ishtar, meaning "star." But if we look closely at the story of Esther, she did not start off like a star. Her Hebrew name was Hadassah, meaning compassion. Compassion is what God used to place this exiled Jewish orphan, who was raised by a man named Mordecai, in the position of royalty and favor. But we know that when God is in the equation, how we start does not define how we finish. He selects people based not on their history, but on His purpose. Regardless of her start, when we read about Esther, she is described as "beautiful beyond all others," and King Xerxes falls in love with her and elevates her above every other woman.

This picture of Esther receiving the royal crown is a powerful one for each of us who may not have had the start in life that we felt we deserved or who have been dealt hardship that seems unfairly off-loaded into our lives. What this image tells us is that our past can't hinder our God-given destiny. Pastor and author Rick Warren said, "We are the product of our past, but we don't have to be a prisoner to it." Regardless of what has happened to us, we don't have to be shackled to it and allow it to define us. But let's be honest: Life can be overwhelming. Even when we're confident and competent in our abilities and skills to achieve success with joy and gratitude, we can attest to the reality that sometimes, life still gets hard. And if we don't stay alert to what we believe to be true about who God is in the middle of every situation, and if we struggle to continue to see His hand in times of trouble, we can become chained to lies, tricks, and schemes designed to distort our value and worth in the middle of our story, sabotaging the potential for our ending.

What are the chains in our life that can cause us to get stuck? They could be addictions, hurts, broken relationships, unforgiveness, or a painful past. And although we could shuffle around while wearing these chains, we would tire easily from the emotional, mental, physical, and spiritual weight. Those chains would shift our walk, our ability to connect, our attitude on life, our interactions, our habits, and our behaviors. We see women all around us—in church, at work, in our homes, at social events—with these chains on. Some are visible, and others are invisible.

Some chains are not as obvious when they are locked on due to life circumstances and situations. You can't see the shackled thoughts that may arise from a past riddled with adversity or patterns of disappointments, but our minds are often hijacked by toxic thoughts such as:

You're not ...
smart enough,
spiritual enough,
pretty enough ...
fill-in-the-blank enough.

The same is true about the hurt that comes from emotional wounds of betrayal, rejection, and abandonment: You can't see them, but the chains are still there. We know that God is concerned about our thoughts because we are urged in Romans 12 to renew the way we think so that we can know the will of God. God also promises us in Psalm 147:3 that *He heals the brokenhearted and binds up their wounds (curing their pains and sorrows)*. If we're honest, all of us could admit there are times when we struggle with wrong thoughts and the unhealthy emotions they create. Their impact on life, relationships, beliefs, and behaviors is the same: Shackled!

Encountering others can confirm, affirm, or shift my belief system of my right to be sentenced with these chains or entitled to live freely and abundantly.

What might you think about a woman walking in her chains?

_____
_____
_____
_____

How might you explain her noticeable struggles?

_____
_____
_____
_____
_____

What might you say about her to yourself or to others?

_____
_____
_____
_____
_____

Would you be empathetic or judgmental because her chains look different from your own?

_____

_____

_____

_____

Let's imagine for a moment that a woman such as that is in our midst today. What can we say to her to encourage her? Jot down what you would say to her to encourage her to drop her chains.

_____

_____

_____

_____

Now, I want you to imagine that you are this woman and to look through her lens to see how she might perceive these messages. If we reached for the scratched lenses we discussed in the F.E.A.R. chapter and wore those glasses, we would see this woman looking through the scratches of her past. With those lenses on, what you're seeing is her vision of her life; it's distorted. Therefore, any messages delivered, good or bad, become distorted. She is not able to receive them clearly, without the marks and scrapes of her past.

Ladies, we need each other because this journey requires endurance. Individually and together, we want to let go of everything that has shrouded us in darkness and exercise patience with ourselves and one another as we deliberately polish our lenses and move away from places of bondage and embrace the freedom that awaits us.

Letting go of our chains (thoughts/hurts) is essential to becoming everything God has called us to be. It means placing our toxic thoughts and unresolved pain at the foot of the cross, where grace and suffering meet. Sometimes, letting go is difficult because we don't physically see the chains, so we deny them or ignore them because they are too difficult to acknowledge or confront. It's also possible that we don't make clear connections that our unhealthy thought patterns and unresolved emotional pain were born out of or from our past or childhood experiences.

Awareness: Rewrite Your Story

ISAIAH 43:18–19 (MSG) *"Forget about what's happened; don't keep going over old history. Be alert, be present. I'm about to do something brand-new. It's bursting out! Don't you see it? There it is! I'm making a road through the desert, rivers in the badlands."*

Something in your past or even present situation might be contributing to unhealthy thoughts and emotions. It has in some way become a barrier in your journey of becoming all God has called you to be.

These messages we believe are like old tapes skewed with lies and based on "false truths" that were voices from our past or perhaps still are being reinforced and validated by the voices of individuals in our lives today. The beauty of tapes is that you can erase them or tape over them. (I know I am dating myself, but you get the point!) You, too, have the power to rewrite the message or create a new meaning statement and make a choice today to believe it. You have the power to write a new truth to your story and create the neuro connections that forge a pathway in your brain to believe it. This is similar to when my daughter is jolted awake from a bad dream and comes to tell me about it. To help her address the nightmare, I'll ask her to tell me how she would change the ending of the dream. Sometimes she'll describe how she would rewrite the ending with herself as the one in control overtaking the fear, the situation, or the character that tried to devastate her. She takes control, and she's no longer the victim but now the victor. She writes an entirely new ending for her brain to accept.

Words are powerful, and even more powerful is the meaning we assign to them. We know this because Proverbs 18:21 tells us: *Life and death are in the power of the tongue.*

Using index cards to create new meanings can be a new habit you develop as you journey in becoming a Woman who is called by God and who is enough. With the help of the Holy Spirit and God's word, you have the power to speak life to yourself. For each Scripture passage below, write a message about who you are as the victor in the middle of your story.

EPHESIANS 2:10 (NIV) *For we are God's handiwork, created in Christ Jesus to do good works, which God prepared in advance for us to do.*

_____

_____

_____

_____

ISAIAH 64:8 (NIV) *Yet you, Lord, are our Father. We are the clay, you are the potter; we are all the work of your hand.*

_____

_____

_____

PSALM 139:14 (NIV) *I praise you because I am fearfully and wonderfully made; your works are wonderful, I know that full well.*

_____

_____

_____

PSALM 46:5 (NIV) *God is within her, she will not fall; God will help her at break of day.*

_____

_____

_____

_____

PSALM 28:7 (NIV) *The Lord is my strength and my shield; my heart trusts in him, and he helps me. My heart leaps for joy, and with my song I praise him.*

_____

_____

_____

_____

LUKE 1:45 (NIV) *"Blessed is she who has believed that the Lord would fulfill his promises to her!"*

_____

_____

_____

_____

1 PETER 3:3–4 (NIV) *Your beauty should not come from outward adornment, such as elaborate hairstyles and the wearing of gold jewelry or fine clothes. Rather, it should be that of your inner self, the unfading beauty of a gentle and quiet spirit, which is of great worth in God's sight.*

_____

_____

_____

_____

Rewriting hurtful messages replaces bitterness with sweetness and heals our bodies, according to Proverbs 16:24: *Gracious words are like honeycomb, sweetness to the soul and health to the body.*

As a woman of God, you have every right to fully experience *your* destiny. Although you can't change your past or what happened yesterday, you have the power through the Holy Spirit to change, to create new meaning out of your experiences. Ephesians 4:23 says, *Be made new in the attitudes of your minds.* In this Scripture, "new" means to put off the former way of life and be renewed in the spirit of your mind, which is the likeness of God created in righteousness and holiness.

"We must choose to believe what God says about who we are and who we were created to be; otherwise, we entertain the lies planted in the soil of our past," says my friend Deb Studevan. "Choose to believe God and remember, 'You don't have to seek anyone's approval for the life God has given you to live.'"

The truth is we all have chains—something or someone that is prohibiting our journey of walking freely into our God-ordained destiny. There's no quick fix or magical intervention for getting free from chains; rather, it's a process of utterly surrendering our heart, mind, and self to God, who is our refuge. It's trusting that Christ, our redeemer who is sitting at the right hand of the Father, is interceding on our behalf. That interceding is what placed Esther at the feet of a king to receive her crown and, in a moment, shift her destiny, not only in her eyes but in the eyes of her people.

Understanding: Who You Are Designed to Be

EPHESIANS 1:11–12 (MSG) *It's in Christ that we find out who we are and what we are living for. Long before we first heard of Christ and got our hopes up, He had his eye on us, had designs on us for glorious living, part of the overall purpose He is working out in everything and everyone.*

Let's return to Esther's story. In Esther chapter 4, she has a conversation with the man who knows her the best and has raised her, Mordecai. In it, Esther's past shows up to collide with her present and destroy her future, or so she thought.

After the nobleman Haman (hater of the Jews) convinces King Xerxes to annihilate all the Jews in his kingdom, Mordecai returns to Esther to ask for her help. The royal eunuchs inform Esther of Mordecai's devastating news for all of her people and relay his request that she go before the king to beg for the mercy of her people.

But Esther hesitates in meeting the request and replies with an excuse.

Why does she hesitate? After all, these were her people.

She had not revealed to the king that she was a Jew. Could she have paused from the fear, the shame of her past, the threat of disclosure, the jeopardy that her present may collapse in the shadow of her past? Was there a way she could escape? She was making the classic mistake of underestimating God's purpose because it did not fit her current plan. Remember that God does not pick people because of their past; He picks them because of His purpose.

Her eyes were more focused on her situation than on her "predestined purpose." We get confused at times and think our elevation is about us—until something comes along that shakes our foundation. Esther needed a reminder that she did not get to the palace on her own. God's Purpose placed her there. The palace may have been her current platform, but God orchestrated her destiny for this divine moment. And Mordecai, sensing her hesitation, reminds her of this.

ESTHER 4:12–14 (MSG) *When Hathach (the eunuch) told Mordecai what Esther had said, Mordecai sent her this message: "Don't think that just because you live in the king's house, you're the one Jew who will get out of this alive. If you persist in staying silent at a time like this, help and deliverance will arrive for the Jews from someplace else; but you and your family will be wiped out. Who knows? Maybe you were made queen for just such a time as this."*

From the very inception of *our* being as women, God has looked at us and our lives as an architect looks at the design of a building. God was Esther's architect, but what does an architect do? He does not actually lay the bricks or drive the bulldozer, but he lays out the details by which the type of brick, cement, and beams are decided upon to determine how much weight the building can bear.

Esther forgot that she was a designer's original.

The Divine Architect designed:

her will

her strength

her personality

her tenacity

her beauty

her intellect.

He designed each building element—all to determine what she's able to bear, and it all will be used for His purpose. In very much the same way, He is preparing you for what he has prepared for you.

Think further about the importance of an architect: You cannot wait until the weight is placed on the building before designing its construction. You design the construction before the weight has ever been applied. So when the architect is asked, "Can the building bear the weight?" he does not guess what the building can bear. He *knows* what it is designed to carry.

Likewise, God knows what Esther is able to bear, and He knows what you are able to do, because there is purpose in your Divine design and construction. Mordecai had to remind her why God had put her there in the first place.

The Architect's design has stood true to the weight, and He knows how much you, like Esther, have had to bear. When faced with a great weight, Esther must believe more in the architect than the load and walk boldly into a fearless conversation in order to forge her destiny and that of her people. So she says,

ESTHER 4:16 (NKJV) *"Go and gather together all the Jews of Susa and fast for me. Do not eat or drink for three days, night or day. My maids and I will do the same. And then, though it is against the law, I will go in to see the king. If I must die, I must die."*

If we look closely, we see that Mordecai's request has made Esther vulnerable before the king, and it also has exposed her past. God's plan has created the platform to put her on display. The very identity that she was hiding from is the thumbprint He is using to connect things from her past to validate her present. He is connecting the story she was ashamed of with the story of her present to create new chapters for the future of *all* of her people. Esther is the only one with the heritage and the heart to impact both sides of the issue. By being both a Jew and now royalty, she's in the unique position to have influence over the outcome because she sees the urgency of both perspectives. No one else could be used in this moment in just the same way to create the needed action that would impact generations to come. She was out on display for His purpose, not hers. Likewise, He will pull the cloak of shame off of our lives and use the very thing we are hiding behind, under, or in to shout to the world, *"She is enough,* and watch how I use everything for her good!"

Exactly as He did with Esther, as the Architect of our design, He knows what you can bear and why you were constructed in the first place to bless you and make you a blessing.

Go to the Fearless Conversations with a Limitless God Video Companion at https://gumroad.com/livingstrongllc#. (Enter the discount code m88hm52 to access the video content for free.) Then watch our "Iron Sharpens Iron" Fearless Conversations video. Listen as these women share their personal stories of shaping identity, and then answer the following questions. What is God revealing to you about the ability to use your story and finding value in how He will continue to find value in you and use you?

How do our beliefs about our value impact our bold, abundant life in Christ?

_____

_____

_____

_____

What is the connection between self-acceptance and self-care?

_____

_____

_____

_____

How can identifying broken patterns and habits associated with a lack of confidence unlock a door to fearless, tenacious faith and our destiny?

_____

_____

_____

_____

What are some action steps for building confidence, self-acceptance, and trust in the faithfulness of God as our maker and creator?

_____

_____

_____

_____

What life lessons have you learned about the power of confidence and your walk as a woman of God?

_____

_____

_____

_____

Take Action:
Stepping into Knowing You Are Enough

PSALM 139:13–16 (MSG) _Oh yes, you shaped me first inside, then out; you formed me in my mother's womb. I thank you, High God—you're breathtaking! Body and soul, I am marvelously made! I worship in adoration—what a creation! You know me inside and out, you know every bone in my body; You know exactly how I was made, bit by bit, how I was sculpted from nothing into something. Like an open book, you watched me grow from conception to birth; all the stages of my life were spread out before you, the days of my life all prepared before I'd even lived one day._

One day I found myself sitting across my kitchen table from a friend of mine. In her office, awards for achievements covered the wall. The signature line in her email displayed the letters of degrees behind her name, and she could legitimately boast of her ability to accomplish more in the first four hours of her day than most people can achieve in an entire day. At work, she had earned the leadership position that so many others coveted. Yet on this particular morning, she sat across from me in tears, unable to even lift the cup of coffee that I offered her.

She was struggling because the position, the title, and the platform upon which she had based her identity had recently crumbled around her. The accolades that she had once used to define her value had turned into unwarranted criticism. Her pain was so palpable that it was almost as if the shattered pieces of a dream lay scattered across my kitchen table, along with the position, job, and title she thought she needed.

As we wrestled with the tension of her white-knuckle grip

around this seeming failure, we were forced to grapple with the question, "What do you do when everything you thought you knew gets shaken?"

I haven't shared my friend's name, because her identity is not as relevant as the pervasiveness of her story. Many of us confuse who we are with what we do and have traded purpose and identity for a "platform of performance." Those moments stain my own memory, and I have met many women who, behind the curtain of their achievements, struggle to believe that they are enough and that they have enough. When that platform is shaken, our identity topples along with our nice, neat plans and the vision of how things should look.

It's not who we are that holds us back but instead who we believe we're not that does. And what we believe about what our God can do with the pieces of our story places a lock on our minds to the Potential, Providence, and Placement of God's hand on the outcome.

God has the ability to take every piece of your life and make it work for good. I think of it like baking! Have you ever tried a teaspoon of baking powder all by itself? HORRIBLE! All by itself it is really bad, but mixed with other ingredients ...

Being poor can leave a bad taste in your mouth ... by itself.

Being an outcast Jew can leave a bad taste in your mouth ... by itself.

Being viewed as a less-than woman can leave a bad taste in your mouth ... by itself.

But mixed together? Similar to the mixed ingredients of a cake: baking powder, eggs, milk, flour, and it starts the process ... for something amazing!

Notice, though, that I said "starts the process," because this mixture still requires some heat! When we trust God and allow Him to place us in heated situations, the plan will come fully together! You can't outthink or out-plan God's providence. And when those ingredients are finally taken out of the oven at "just the right time," they yield a product that glorifies the Master Baker and shows the world, "Oh, taste and see that the Lord is mmm, mmm good!"

ESTHER 8:11–15 (NIV) *The king's edict granted the Jews in every city the right to assemble and protect themselves; to destroy, kill, and annihilate the armed men of any nationality or province who might attack them and their women and children, and to plunder the property of their enemies. The day appointed for the Jews to do this in all the provinces of King Xerxes was the thirteenth day of the twelfth month, the month of Adar. A copy of the text of the edict was to be issued as law in every province and made known to the people of every nationality so that the Jews would be ready on that day to avenge themselves on their enemies. The couriers, riding the royal horses, went out, spurred on by the king's command, and the edict was issued in the citadel of Susa. When Mordecai left the king's presence, he was wearing royal garments of blue and white, a large crown of gold, and a purple robe of fine linen. And the city of Susa held a joyous celebration. For the Jews it was a time of happiness and joy, gladness and honor. In every province and in every city to which the edict of the king came, there was joy and gladness among the Jews, with feasting and celebrating. And many people of other nationalities became Jews because fear of the Jews had seized them.*

How do we survive the heating process to get to the provision?

Get clear about who you are. In your quiet time, ask yourself, "Who am I?" Then wait for the answer to rise to the surface. Tasks, activities, or descriptions from other people may float up first. Toss those out and wait for the thoughts that bring a smile to your face. Start writing them down. The words will inspire and motivate you when you think of them. They may also make you uncomfortable when you say them back to yourself in the mirror, because they may be a *truth* that you seldom hear but are desperate to believe. Post the list and keep adding to it over days and months. Every time God brings a statement of value and identity of who He says you are, add it to the list.

Get rid of the lies that others have told you about who they think you are. I had a conversation with a woman who was struggling to obtain a position that would finally allow her to fully provide for her single-parent family. I asked her what she loved to do, and she responded with a few descriptors. Then she quickly followed them with the statement, "But I am a slow learner, and it takes me a while to get things right." In that moment she revealed a true barrier to her success: her mindset. With the voice of motivational speaker Lisa Nichols in my head, I asked, "Who told you that lie, and when did you decide to believe it?" She paused, shocked that I would ask such a question, because we had just met. Then she cast her gaze to the floor as she realized that she had no idea when it began, but that for her entire life she had believed that narrative about herself.

What if who we said we want to be is who we actually believed we are on the inside? Write down each lie that you have told yourself, and then write a parallel truth statement about who you know you actually are. Say the list to yourself in the mirror every morning for the next 30 days.

_____

_____

_____

_____

Get free of unwanted baggage that comes from unforgiveness for others, for situations, and for yourself. We choose to carry the baggage of unforgiveness. Forgiveness is not an event; it is a process. It may begin for you as the process of decisional forgiveness, which is the conscious decision to actively practice forgiving another person or yourself. It rests on the surface and may feel awkward and operational at first, but it has a clear purpose. The act of decisional forgiveness creates a habit that becomes a part of you. It allows you to think about what you believe to be true and consciously decide to no longer carry the burden to be free. You see, forgiveness is not saying the person had the right to do anything they did. Yes, it was wrong, and yes, it hurt! Forgiveness is proclaiming that the hurt will no longer define who you are. Forgiveness is about setting *you* free. In the process of getting free, you can begin to move into emotional forgiveness, which is emotionally unlocking the chain of being bound to the person, place, or past mistakes. Emotional forgiveness allows you to make the shift of forgiveness at an emotional level, within your motivations, emotions, thoughts, and memories. Both decisional and emotional forgiveness are a journey and a process that is engaged in over time, but we must be willing to make the time and invest in the process.

Check out our Pursuit Cards in our eStore for visual daily reminders of how to break broken patterns and live life to the fullest ... and running over ☺! https://gumroad.com/livingstrongllc#

Rest in Reflection: What Has God Revealed to You?

How can your responses and reactions change in situations with a greater awareness that you are enough?

_____

_____

_____

_____

_____

_____

Take some time for focused reflection and intentional celebration. Review your journal or notes from the last chapter. What are your top three takeaways from this experience?

_____

_____

_____

Why did those things stand out to you?

_____

_____

_____

Mind. Body. Soul. Connection: Now let's restore some mental pathways through the therapeutic activity of coloring. Take this time to connect worship, prayer, music, and stillness while you focus on the creative act of coloring. Coloring has been found to reduce anxiety, increase focus, build awareness, and provide clarity. When you take the time to calm your mind, your brain enters a relaxed state by focusing on the present and blocking out the nonstop thinking we all experience. As a result, you reach a place of calm that relieves your brain from the daily stresses of life and allows you to continue to refresh and restore. So find your favorite worship song and a quiet place to sit, and let's start coloring.

PSALM 17:8 (NKJV) *Keep me as the apple of Your eye; Hide me under the shadow of Your wings.*

The Revelation of Gratitude

LUKE 21:1–4 (NKJV) *And He looked up and saw the rich putting their gifts into the treasury, and He saw also a certain poor widow putting in two mites. So He said, "Truly I say to you that this poor widow has put in more than all; for all these out of their abundance have put in offerings for God, but she out of her poverty put in all the livelihood that she had."*

Basement: Gratitude Is a Heart Condition

Have you ever had one of those moments when God makes you pause or stop in your tracks so that you can *really* get something He is trying to teach you? This verse and repeated interactions during my day yesterday did that for me. More than once yesterday, God showed me that out of obedience and gratitude His work is not only done but multiplied, and that gratitude does not hinge on the character, behavior, or actions of others but the condition of my heart.

Understanding why a widow would donate all she had to live on begins not with what was in her pocket but what was in her heart. How often does our perception of our "not enough" prevent us from really accessing God's "more than enough"? As I read commentary after commentary on this image of a widow giving two mites, I observed that there were many views taken. Some commentators focused on the standard of giving sacrificially, condemnation of the mindset and religious officials of the day that profited from the poor, the picture of social inequity, or the imbalance in the religious, political, and social structures of the day. While all of that may have a place, I actually just want to focus on the heart of the widow. Let's rest on the image of a meager woman who woke up that morning alone, again—comforted only by the memories of her husband. She placed her worn cloak on her back, reached in a small container where she had been saving two small coins, and pressed her way forward to give, not out of her abundance but out of her lack. But was it only lack?

Jesus said she "… put in all the livelihood that she had" (Luke 21:4). Hmmm … to give all she had for her *livelihood* suggests this widow must have seen her abundance beyond worldly possessions, because Christ didn't say she gave *all that she had*. She gave from all she had to live on, but was she able to do that because she knew that those two coins did not represent *all* of her significance and did not reflect the full abundance of her life? As a widow, especially during this time in history, she had experienced her fair share of loss. I can attest from my own experience of loss and pain that it is these moments when I have been pushed into a place of seeking God's grace that would have never happened without the weight of the hurt or pain taking me there. And it is in that place that God has met me and given me the treasures of peace, hope, sound mind, forgiveness, wholeness, fortitude, and assurance.

I can honestly say that without the pain I would not have ever experienced that level of grace or accessed the plans He predestined for me. In that place of loss, a revelation of His grace birthed my gratitude for His love that no price tag could measure. It makes me wonder if this widow could relate to that place and knew of this grace. I wonder if she was able to see past what she did not have to what she still had to offer and had received, and she was grateful for it, so she gave? Perhaps you can think of ways you might be grateful in spite of your loss.

Think through some things you have that no one can take away and write them below.

_____

_____

_____

_____

_____

Fearless Conversations with a Limitless God

Historians describe the backdrop of a corrupt system, the twisted hearts of others, and a greedy social structure, and this widow still offered what she had to live off of because she knew there was more sustaining her than those two mites. When we are able to shift our gaze to the revelation of what we *still* have in spite of the plots and schemes that have tried to rise up from our background, it deepens our awareness of an abundance that doesn't rest in just the physical.

Tamara Levitt from the meditation app "Calm" shares a definition of gratitude that made we wonder about the heart, strength, and fortitude of this "poor widow": "Gratitude is the practice of waking up in order to see the good all around us." Could our true abundance, and the abundance of this widow, rise not from what we see in our hand but from the view we see from our inner resilience created from a default setting of gratitude, humility, love, and peace?

That mindset pushes us to move away from the oversimplified perspective of "Get it! Grab it! Gratitude" to one that seeks out gratitude in meaningful ways beyond the grind, comparisons, and wants of life. It forces us to acknowledge that gratitude is not about a mood but rather our mindset and heart position. It challenges us to not place conditions on our position of gratitude, such as when we think, *I'll be grateful when they are treating me better* or *I'll show gratitude when the issue changes.*

In the passage from Luke, many people gave from their tangible abundance as an offering to God and as a show for others. In His conversation and teachable moment with everyone around Him, Jesus notices the widow's giving and does not mention any struggle in the giving of her *last* as her offering of gratitude to her God. He does not mention a pause, a hesitancy, or a reluctance as the coins slipped from her grip—only that she arrived on the scene and gave in the same manner as everyone else. Could this woman have given with such ease from such a place of tangible deficit because her offering, her gratitude to God, was connected to a storehouse of benefits? Could she have known that these benefits would put her in a place of mental, emotional, and spiritual wealth that would sustain her life in entirely different ways than the people and crooked scribes with tangible wealth could ever understand?

Awareness: The Mind of Gratitude

God tells us that "my ways are not your ways," and if you just bring me the little you have in a heart of obedience and gratitude, I will do *much* with it for my glory to save, restore, repair, and reconcile many.

Whatever is in your hand today, know that it is enough! Show your gratitude for it, offer it in obedience, and watch what happens. He will take the things you might think to be insignificant, not really good enough, or too small to really matter much and use every ounce of them to bless others over and over again when you give out of obedience, love for Him, and gratitude.

Our peace is wrapped in our gratitude. In Philippians 4:6–7 (ESV), we read, *In everything by prayer and supplication with thanksgiving let your requests be made known to God. And the peace of God, which surpasses all understanding, will guard your hearts and your minds in Christ Jesus.* Science places a tangible exclamation mark on this Biblical principle. Research study after research study has shown the psychological, physical, and social benefits of gratitude in improving our feelings of joy, our social connections with others, our immune system, our mental capacity, and our blood pressure.

The practice of gratitude literally rewires the brain and renews the mind (Romans 12:2 NIV). It counterbalances the natural nature of our brains to be hyper-focused on the negative, dangerous, and threatening experiences of life out of a survival instinct. The brain is wired to know what is negative to protect us in those key moments of danger, so the practice of gratitude opens our minds to more than survival to access the opportunity to thrive in a broader awareness that we are not solely dependent on our capacity. As Philippians 4:6 states, placing our safety, needs, and requests in the hands of our God can give our minds security and a platform for gratitude in a God we trust will provide. The practice of shifting our focus to this place of gratitude in a Sovereign God won't always make sense, but it will unlock our hearts and minds to a door of peace beyond our understanding. However, that requires a conscious practice of guarding our heart and mind, or, specifically, our thoughts. The thoughts we feed ourselves daily will fuel the wiring that takes place in our brains. Neuropsychologist Donald Hebb says, "Neurons that fire together wire together." In other words, whichever thoughts we feed ourselves the most will connect the most, so the act of crushing complaining and cultivating gratitude requires daily, intentional habit. Philippians 4:6 gives practical steps of creating a choice each day to rewire habits of negativity and instead live our lives with thankfulness and joy. The choice is always ours. But it requires us to open our awareness, wakening our intentional focus from discontent, comparison, and distorted expectations to a perspective of what we actually still have in our lives. Let's look at how we can reframe our perspective:

What relationships can you be grateful for?

_____

_____

_____

_____

Is there anything you are taking for granted that you actually could become grateful for, if you looked more closely?

_____

_____

_____

_____

What challenges have you been faced with? What did you learn, and how can you be thankful for the experiences?

_____

_____

_____

_____

What opportunities or privileges do you have that you could be thankful for?

_____

_____

_____

_____

How can you thank God and others more often?

_____

_____

_____

Understanding: Feeling Frustrated or Disappointed?

It isn't that we shouldn't have high expectations, or that we shouldn't feel hurt when someone lets us down. But one of the best ways to recover from disappointment is to notice what actually is going well in our lives.

1 THESSALONIANS 5:18 (NLT) *Be thankful in all circumstances, for this is God's will for you who belong to Christ Jesus.*

This passage tells us when we are to be thankful and why. This is God's will for all of us because He knows that a grateful heart leads to a fruitful life. Gratitude is a skill, like learning to ride a bike or learning a new language. It can be taught, and it needs to be practiced consciously and deliberately. In the conversation above, Paul explains the instructions for the heart and head knowledge of true gratitude. Grateful people focus less on what is missing and more on the opportunity that can come out of every situation.

When I was an aspiring leader in my career, my boss at the time told me, "Every experience, good or bad, opens a door to opportunity based on which way you turn the key. You can lock yourself in or unlock your threshold moment." I have never forgotten that aha moment, and it shifted how I viewed every struggle in business moving forward.

But the statement can apply to much more than work. Grateful people reflect on blessings instead of rehearsing their expectations. Replaying what we think we deserve, should have received, or should not have experienced gets us stuck in the "shoulda trap" and clouds our vision from discovering God's hand still on the move. Our enemy would want nothing better than to have us rehearse disappointments and miss God's accomplishments and His nature to be a giver, provider, protector, and source for more. We must shift our eyes to look for Him and not the disappointment.

Go to the Fearless Conversations with a Limitless God Video Companion at https://gumroad.com/livingstrongllc#. (Enter the discount code m88hm52 to access the video content for free.) Then watch our "Iron Sharpens Iron" Fearless Conversations video. Listen as these women share their personal stories of pain, victory, and revelation, and then answer the following questions. What is God revealing to you about being fearless and cultivating a life-style of gratitude on purpose?

How has a lack of gratitude influenced your behavior and decisions?

_____

_____

_____

_____

What are some of the reasons we aren't as grateful as we should be?

_____

_____

_____

_____

How do gratitude and faithfulness fuel each other?

_____

_____

_____

_____

What are some ways to cultivate gratitude in your daily life?

_____

_____

_____

_____

What life lessons have you learned about the power of gratitude?

_____

_____

_____

_____

Action Steps to Replace Worry
with Worship and Unlock a Habit of Gratitude

PHILIPPIANS 4:6–8 (MSG) *Don't fret or worry. Instead of worrying, pray. Let petitions and praises shape your worries into prayers, letting God know your concerns. Before you know it, a sense of God's wholeness, everything coming together for good, will come and settle you down. It's wonderful what happens when Christ displaces worry at the center of your life. Summing it all up, friends, I'd say you'll do best by filling your minds and meditating on things true, noble, reputable, authentic, compelling, gracious—the best, not the worst; the beautiful, not the ugly; things to praise, not things to curse.*

Worship rises from a heart of gratitude. Gratitude looks back at grace and shapes the footsteps for the forward movement toward hope. Build the momentum for these footprints through a daily practice of reflecting on and then writing down three things that represent how grateful you are "in spite of" for the grace found in each passing moment, day, week, and month. You will be surprised at how trading in your worries for gratitude and worship will change your entire perspective on life.

Gratitude Tracking List for 21 days:

Day 1: _____

_____

_____

Day 2: _____

_____

_____

Day 3: _____

_____

_____

Day 4: _____

_____

_____

Day 5: _____

_____

_____

Day 6: _____

_____

_____

Day 7: _____

_____

_____

Day 8: _____

_____

_____

Day 9: _____

_____

_____

Day 10: _____

_____

_____

Day 11: _____

_____

_____

Day 12: _____

_____

_____

Day 13: _____

_____

_____

Day 14: _____

_____

_____

Day 15: _____

_____

_____

Day 16: _____

_____

_____

Day 17: _____

_____

_____

Day 18: _____

_____

_____

Day 19: _____

_____

_____

Day 20: _____

_____

_____

Day 21: _____

_____

_____

Our enemy wants us to forget about all the things we should be thankful for. He wants us vulnerable to attack, so he reminds us constantly of what we have lost, how we are not enough, or what is needed or wanted to be or do more. The intentional practice of guarding our heart builds the safeguards for a mindset of gratitude. Interrupting toxic or destructive thought patterns becomes physically, mentally, and emotionally vital to actually begin to *notice* what we have access to, rather than being hyper-focused on our deficit.

PHILIPPIANS 4:8 (MSG) *I'd say you'll do best by filling your minds and meditating on things true, noble, reputable, authentic, compelling, gracious—the best, not the worst; the beautiful, not the ugly; things to praise, not things to curse.*

This verse instructs us to slow down our thought life and be intentional with what we think about, and also what we meditate on, stew over, play on repeat, and become loyal to in our mindset. Research conducted at Harvard Health and the Greater Good Science Center at UC Berkeley lists the physical shifts our bodies experience when we pause and notice and gain a sharper awareness of what we have access to—not just in our pockets but also in our hearts, souls, and minds. Gratitude sharpens our senses, pulls us out of autopilot for toxic complaining and broken thinking, and opens up our physical wealth in life through improved sleep, reduced pain symptoms, increased relaxation, greater energy, and a healthier heart.

We can use the image of an Emotional First Aid Kit as a reminder to wake up our senses and shift ourselves out of broken patterns, so that we can grab tight to a wellness mindset.

Emotional First Aid Kit

When thoughts arise that you are not enough, don't have enough, or have lost too much, slow down the process and take care of your emotional and mental state.

Imagine reaching for a first aid kit with the usual items that now have powerful properties for emotional healing:

Pain cream: When you are triggered by a situation, memory, or painful scenario, don't just keep going and pretend it didn't impact you. Recognize the sensations that you are feeling in your body—the flushed face, the fast heartbeat, or the pain in your stomach or back. Acknowledge the sensation that will show up in your body before the emotion even takes root. If someone physically wounded you, you would reach for a pain cream to soothe the pain. We may not be able to see emotional wounds, but that doesn't mean they remain invisible. Untreated emotional wounds do not just go away because we ignore the hurt. They show up as repeated pain and unpleasant sensations in our bodies. Become aware of the sensation and treat it with a cooling, calming approach that centers your mind and body: Place your hand on the area that hurts, rub it, and *breathe*. Reach for cold water to encourage your system to calm down. Pay attention to the signals your body gives you.

Thermometer: Assess the situation and degrees of the impact. Ask yourself, "What about this situation created that response in me?" and "What meaning have I attached to this situation?"

Ice pack: As the initial shock wears off, pay attention to the shift in your sensations so that you begin to create muscle memory for what it feels like to be calm and sense healing.

Bandage: Believe in your innate design to heal. Begin to access the word of God to wrap and secure fragile areas with the support of God's truth, healing the wounded areas of your heart.

Compact mirror: Take intentional time to reflect on the truth you have been studying and say it back to yourself. Replace the outdated self-talk with affirming truth.

Rubber band: Acknowledge that God is stretching you and inspiring you to take action. Work on your gratitude journal, create a vision board, or start a thank-you jar. The key thing here is to not stay stuck.

Smelling salts: Aromatherapy, music, lotions, and soft textures are all ways to come back to your five senses and interrupt negative mental patterns. Take time to rest and really meditate on what God has been revealing to you. Don't be afraid to feel the emotions and unpack what they mean. Now, using your senses, connect your mind, body, and spirit to relax and be still. Put on your favorite worship song and allow the words to wash over you in a new way.

Treatment chart: Process your growth. Reframe situations and write down possible new ways to view things, lessons learned, and *in spite of* moments that God has awoken you to about your story. Document your testimony and become a part of the healing process for someone else.

Check out our Action Cards in our eStore for visual daily reminders of how to break broken patterns and live life to the fullest … and running over ☺! www.livingstrongllc.com/eStore

Rest in Reflection: What Has God Revealed to You?

How can your responses and reactions change in situations when you have a greater awareness for gratitude?

_____

_____

_____

Take some time for focused reflection and intentional celebration. Review your journal or notes from this chapter. What are your top three takeaways from this experience?

_____

_____

_____

Why did those things stand out to you?

_____

_____

_____

Mind. Body. Soul. Connection: Now let's restore some mental pathways through the therapeutic activity of coloring. Take this time to connect worship, prayer, music, and stillness while you focus on the creative act of coloring. Coloring has been found to reduce anxiety, increase focus, build awareness, and provide clarity. When you take the time to calm your mind, your brain enters a relaxed state by focusing on the present and blocking out the nonstop thinking we all experience. As a result, you reach a place of calm that relieves your brain from the daily stresses of life and allows you to continue to refresh and restore. So find your favorite worship song and a quiet place to sit, and let's start coloring.

LAMENTATIONS 3:22–24 (ESV) *The steadfast love of the Lord never ceases; his mercies never come to an end; they are new every morning; great is your faithfulness. "The Lord is my portion," says my soul, "therefore I will hope in him."*

Joy with My Soul

Basement: The Wrestling Match

JAMES 1:2–3 (NIV) Consider it pure joy, my brothers and sisters, whenever you face trials of many kinds, because you know that the testing of your faith produces perseverance.

It had been a hard nine months, but God had held my hand the entire way, even on the days I was so angry with Him that I tried to wiggle my hand out of His grip. That may be too honest for some of you, but there were days that I held on to such bitterness all I could do was be angry and yell at God for "letting them treat me like that and get away with it." But as I drove home on this afternoon, I reflected on how thankful I was for a God who could handle my anger. Even through the fallout from my infected emotional wound, He applied healing patience, love, consistency, and the example of a healthy relationship like an antibiotic cream from an Emotional First Aid Kit.

Prior to the healing process of those nine months, I had been hurt by people in the church, and the weapons of their unresolved past showed up in our relationship and left me broken, cut, and confused about my value, identity, and ability to survive. A lot of pain remained from distorted statements such as "If your faith were stronger, you wouldn't be so hurt" and "If you were really faithful, you would ..." and "It's your own fault this is happening." I remember the day I said out loud, "If this is God, I don't need Him or them." My pain and confusion were so heavy they took a toll on my body, mind, emotions, and spirit. After eight years of toxic relationships, poor health, venomous messaging, and a slandered reputation riddled with unwarranted gossip, I stepped out of the church and slipped right into depression and confusion. I had run into a crisis of faith, and years of rituals and traditions did not prepare me for the battle in front of me. But none of it caught my God off guard.

He met me every morning in the recliner I used as my spot to weep in. He met me on the walking path that I used to walk out the mental tapes of hurt that I played on repeat. He met me in the shower as I let my tears mix with the water and tried to drown out the hurt that throbbed through my heart and body, as I wept thinking more about death than life. With every encounter, He met me in the moment. As I battled with Him through hurt emotions, He embraced my wrestling and drew me closer to Him every day. I don't remember the how or the first day I stumbled onto Walk in the Word Ministries, but the Jesus he described was not the God I knew, and I became completely intrigued.

With each Walk in the Word message, I began to replace the broken self-talk during my morning walks. There was something about the message of an authentic, loving God that made me want to know *this* God more. As I look back on that time now, I see God's hand, grace, and favor and His desire for all of us *to know Him for ourselves as fortified in truth, grounded in love, and overflowing in grace.* I discovered that this journey of faith is not about rituals but relationship.

The Holy Spirit continued to move and so did I. I traded my recliner for running shoes, and instead of stuffing down the pain, with God's help, I began to process every lie, hurt, and broken message that I had adopted into my belief system. He fostered a thirst for the truth found between the pages of His word and woven into the fibers of His character. It felt like I was meeting Him for the first time, and just as I would in any brand-new relationship, I made it a point to get to know Him better.

With every stride on the running path, I began to shed weight that I had unknowingly been carrying and struggling with, emotionally and physically. I lost 40 pounds of physical weight I had not even realized I was carrying because the mental baggage occupied my attention. As the cloud lifted and I received counseling spiritually and professionally, it was as though someone had removed scratched lenses that had been distorting my view on life, and for the first time, I could *see!* God had not called me to a life isolated, broken, and unwanted. My story was not done, and it was time for me to get back to living. With my mind on its way to healing, I prayed for a job that would allow every gift He had planted in me to have a place to give Him glory and restore who I needed to believe He saw me to be. It had been nine months. We wrestled. He won, and I was reborn.

The legalistic traditions of religion make the Christian walk seem harsh, rigid, and controlled by rules instead of relationship. How can this perspective of Christ rob us of authentic connection to all God has for His children?

_____

_____

_____

In the midst of difficulty, why is it so important to focus on God instead of the trial?

_____

_____

_____

Life isn't nice and neat, and the Bible is a support system for our messy, difficult, real lives. How do the following passages encourage you in your own spiritual journey?

PSALM 118:5 (NIV) *When hard pressed, I cried to the Lord; he brought me into a spacious place.*

_____

_____

_____

JOHN 14:26 (NIV) *But the Advocate, the Holy Spirit, whom the Father will send in my name, will teach you all things and will remind you of everything I have said to you.*

_____

_____

_____

ROMANS 12:12(ESV) *Rejoice in hope, be patient in tribulation, be constant in prayer.*

_____

_____

_____

_____

Awareness: Finding My Joy

God and I had one of our conversations that morning as I got dressed for my new job. I laugh now, thinking about the negotiation process and how the following words left my lips: "I am going to do this, but I will *never* let anyone back in again. Just do my job! Don't make the same mistake again." It made perfect sense to me, right?! Barricade and protect, that was going to be the battle plan, but when we create barricades to keep life out, it keeps all that God has within us in as well.

My plan seemed to get sabotaged from day one as He dropped me into the most relational and loving group of people I had ever witnessed in a professional environment. *(laugh)* God and I went back to the wrestling mat as I shared, "Didn't you hear my plan?! No relationships. Don't let anyone in. Don't you remember what they did to me in the past?" And with the same patience He always showed in our conversations, He dropped this response into my spirit: "I am doing something new, and I want to use you, if you will let me." I am not kidding, the next day my new boss of about two months called me into her office and said, "You have a lot to offer, gifts and talents, but until you let down that brick wall you are carrying around, they will not have any way to get out." Ouch!

ROMANS 15:13(NIV) *May the God of hope fill you with all joy and peace as you trust in him, so that you may overflow with hope by the power of the Holy Spirit.*

Our God does not want us walking around partially healed. He promises a life of abundance and living full, and that requires us to live wholeheartedly. Living life, now, on the other side of this experience with about a decade of time between the hurt and the healing, I am able to see God's hand moving in such intentional ways to guide and orchestrate the healing He had planned for me. I now see that His plan was designed to allow me to access the joy He also had planned for me to walk out in new ways that would blow my mind and create the platform and premise for us to meet in the pages of this book.

When we deal with a relational God and not just the rituals of man, we are able to access truth and process pain, which leads to freedom. As I take time to break down how God would not just let me place a Band-Aid over my pain but actually took me through an experience of processing the pain and putting it into proper perspective, it reminds me of a very practical process for overcoming adversity, trauma, and distorted mental narratives.

As I reflect on the work of Dr. Judith Herman's stage-based approach to trauma and recovery, I recognize that healing is not an event. It is a journey of stages that must first start by establishing safety and self-regulation. God provides us with comfort through the Holy Spirit (John 14:26). Those mornings when He met me in the recliner or on our walks created an intentional process of establishing safety, stability, and regulation for my mind and body to become grounded. During that same time, He provided me with tangible relationships with a few trusted women who knew the Word and shared their relationship with God with me. Through spiritual and physical relationships, I was able to trade in my chaotic thoughts of abandonment for ones of safety and security that rested on a foundation of love and trust.

With a platform of safety in place, the next stage of healing includes mourning whatever loss was experienced by the hurt endured. Just pretending to forget bad memories, sugarcoating hurt, or stuffing pain down creates the toxin that infects the emotional wounds left by damaging relationships. Become brave enough to lean into the pain of memories. Find a trusted counselor or support system to process memories that keep playing on repeat, because the tape won't shut itself off. You will have to reach for that knob yourself. Become attuned to your body and aware of how intrusive thoughts are invading your daily experiences. The daily messages in Walk in the Word kept pointing me back to truth found in the Word of God.

As the enemy would try to attack my thought life with toxic memories, the tangible act of renewing my mind became a daily practice. This meant not running from the memories, but comparing them with the truth of God's plan for me. I journaled often to release my mind of hurtful events but always integrated the step of closing with written statements that rewired my brain and thought life with *how God saw me and my future.* This allowed me to begin to see myself differently and, more importantly, see my relationship with God with new eyes. With a grounded routine of safety and gaining clarity, I could begin to seek out the process of regaining my worth, my impact, and my creativity, recognizing that I am lovable and capable of more.

Reconnecting with my value brought me to the crossroads of needing to decide if my freedom was more valuable to me than the badge of honor I had polished from surviving the hurt I endured. It was time to decide between forgiveness and bitterness. I had become bitter and angry for so many years that I was comfortable with my bitterness, but it was robbing me of my inheritance of joy. In stage three of the process, God offered me the opportunity to connect with the creativity He embedded in me. It was time to offer the world an authentic version of me, not the false facade placed on me from the broken messages of others.

I began to do things that ignited the creative side of me. This creative expression allowed me to integrate my mind, body, and emotions to share the lessons He taught me during those long walks. When I began exploring creative interests during my healing process, areas of my brain that were once stunted by irregular emotions and disruptive thought patterns were able to become active again.

Through creative expression during this third stage, a person can begin to explore their emotions on a deeper level, which gives them more insight and creates mental space for healing to take place. In addition to creating pathways for unresolved emotions, creativity also has the potential to help us increase our focus, work through shame, reduce stress, and improve our work performance.

I wish I could say the stages of this process were linear, easy, and neat, but they weren't. I found myself back in stage one at times just trying to regulate my emotions and figure out what safety really meant to me, or I found myself in stage two wrestling with flashbacks of fear, anger, and frustration. But God provided Divine appointments with every morning conversation over His word or in people he brought into my path to just remind me of the steps He is ordering for my future.

The key to this fearless process was consistency. I call it a fearless process not because there was never any fear, but because in the face of fear, failures, and setbacks, I got back up and fought back for what I wanted (over and over) and for what I was entitled to as a daughter of a King. In this experience, the definition for Fearless was not one that denied the presence of fear or a recklessness with no fear, but it characterized fearless in my life as resolute, courageous, lionhearted, and bold, because it was time.

What are three challenges you have that keep you from accessing the joy you are entitled to?

_____

_____

_____

_____

Why is it important that we not only pray, but also redirect our thoughts of worry?

_____

_____

_____

_____

Understanding: It Is Well with My Soul

ROMANS 14:17–18 (MSG) *God's kingdom isn't a matter of what you put in your stomach, for goodness' sake. It's what God does with your life as he sets it right, puts it together, and completes it with joy. Your task is to single-mindedly serve Christ. Do that and you'll kill two birds with one stone: pleasing the God above you and proving your worth to the people around you.*

What is the difference between happiness and joy?

_____

_____

_____

_____

_____

Happiness is a fleeting emotion that can change with the circumstances or experiences that we have, but joy is a state of mind to be practiced and cultivated. Happiness and joy are both found in the Bible and are used to describe ways of living, but joy is listed as a fruit of the spirit that is planted in the soul (Galatians 5:22–23).

The fruits of the spirit are the unchanging character traits of God. They are offered to us as character traits that provide consistency in our Christlike lifestyle to give us stability in our encounters with people or circumstances, regardless of the ebb and flow of life. The fruits of the spirit come directly from the Holy Spirit to smooth out our rough patches in life, as we learn to abide in the consistent nature of God. Joy is offered as an exchange of our roller-coaster emotions for the temperament of God, creating an intensity to our state of being and our knowledge of who God is and who He is in our circumstances. It is God's joy, temperance, and love for us that infuses our state of being to aid us during our struggles.

Our battles in life are real, and if the enemy can strip us of our joy, he has access to our peace. When we are not single-minded in our pursuit of Him and pay more attention to the struggles and stress in our lives than the joy our God has for us, we start a cascade of toxic responses that create broken cycles that cloud our understanding that we can stay connected to joy because God is for us, not against us. We must know His character and His hand. This creates the template for how we respond to life because we know ultimately our triumph rests in a God who _is_ love and joy. The very act and benefit of trading our worry for His joy can be found in:

PHILIPPIANS 4:6–8 (MSG) *Don't fret or worry. Instead of worrying, pray. Let petitions and praises shape your worries into prayers, letting God know your concerns. Before you know it, a sense of God's wholeness, everything coming together for good, will come and settle you down. It's wonderful what happens when Christ displaces worry at the center of your life.*

Summing it all up, friends, I'd say you'll do best by filling your minds and meditating on things true, noble, reputable, authentic, compelling, gracious—the best, not the worst; the beautiful, not the ugly; things to praise, not things to curse. Put into practice what you learned from me, what you heard and saw and realized. Do that, and God, who makes everything work together, will work you into his most excellent harmonies.

What are you cultivating in your life that is causing you joy?

_____

_____

_____

_____

For me, it became my worship. The practice of my praise in dance became the conduit to a state of accessing joy. Even when the circumstances around me did not change, God could give me a peace and knowing that His hand was still present. My worship provides the fertile ground for my joy to grow in and become a deeper part of me.

When the enemy can take his best shot at me and get me to my knees, but from my knees I can raise my hands, he's got nothing in his arsenal that can combat that. It's a spirit that just won't quit because my state of being is rooted deeper than my circumstances. That grounding, that type of footing, reminds me of the spirit that must have resided in Horatio Spafford when he put pen to paper to write the hymn lyrics "It Is Well with My Soul." Spafford lost his young son to pneumonia in 1871 and, that same year, lost his wealth in the Great Chicago Fire. Two years later, he lost all four of his daughters in a tragic shipwreck. In his voyage to meet his grieving wife in Europe, he begins to write the following words:

When peace like a river, attendeth my way,
When sorrows like sea billows roll,
Whatever my lot, thou hast taught me to say,
It is well, it is well, with my soul

It is well
With my soul
It is well, it is well with my soul

Though Satan should buffet,
though trials should come,
Let this blessed assurance control,
That Christ has regarded my helpless estate,
And hath shed His own blood for my soul

It is well (it is well)
With my soul (with my soul)
It is well, it is well with my soul

My sin, oh, the bliss of this glorious thought
My sin, not in part but the whole,
Is nailed to the cross, and I bear it no more,
Praise the Lord, praise the Lord, O my soul

It is well (it is well)
With my soul (with my soul)
It is well, it is well with my soul

It is well (it is well)
With my soul (with my soul)
It is well, it is well with my soul

That state of being does not come from the emotion of happiness. It comes from a root system of joy. Seeking that kind of core belief requires a lifestyle of cultivating the fruits of the spirit and tilling the soil in our lives.

Go to the Fearless Conversations with a Limitless God Video Companion at https://gumroad.com/livingstrongllc#. (Enter the discount code m88hm52 to access the video content for free.) Then watch our "Iron Sharpens Iron" Fearless Conversations video. Listen as these women share their life lessons on a life of joy. Then reflect on your answers to the questions below. What is God revealing to you about your state of joy?

No one takes our joy from us. We choose whether we will give it away because of situations, circumstances, memories, or sin or whether we will cultivate it because of its power and value in our lives. Can you think of some ways that Satan seeks to steal your joy?

_____

_____

_____

How have you learned the difference between happiness and joy?

_____

_____

_____

What triggers repeat themselves and hinder our access to joy?

_____

_____

_____

When you think of joyful people, what characteristics do they possess?

_____

_____

_____

What life lessons can be used to help you understand the power of your joy and increase your trust in the sovereignty of God—even when His plan does not match your own?

_____

_____

_____

_____

Action Plan

The drive was smooth. The weather was good. And all felt well with my soul. I was reflecting on God's favor and his goodness. The gift of the position He gave me created a safe place for me to cultivate healthy relationships again and gave me time and life balance to pursue things that brought me joy. I had even become aware of a new talent for designing professional development programs that helped adults understand concepts in new ways and brought fun to the adult principles of learning. It was in this moment that I uttered the words, "Thank you, God, for all you have given me, but I want _everything_ you have planned for me. Feel free to use me."

In that moment, I could hear the instruction that it was time to go back to the church that had created so much pain in me years before, because He had an assignment waiting for me there. I will be honest: I almost stopped my car and said, "Devil get out of my car, because that could _not_ possibly be the voice of God!" I can laugh now, but it was not funny then. The words that came to my spirit next have been the driving force for every decision I make when engaging with people today. It was clear in my heart and mind as the words, _"You are to be love and light wherever I send you."_

But they never said they were sorry, Lord. How can I go back?

I have already healed those wounds and given you the spirit of forgiveness. You are no longer shackled to that pain.

But what if they hurt me again?

You are not the same woman you were. Your identity is not hinged on their approval but instead to my grace.

Lord, there has to be a better way!

Do you want EVERYTHING, or not?

Ouch! It took me months after that experience in the car to build the courage to return. But I did go back, and it was in that place of obedience that God provided the opportunity for me to teach my first Women's Sunday School class, and in the middle of the place I was scared to be in and felt vulnerable to stay in, God introduced me to my passion and purpose. Preparing lessons every week for women to access a knowing of the God I got to know on those morning walks became the joy of my week. Creating new and creative ways to present concepts from the Bible in ways that allowed women to understand His character, His love, and His grace more deeply gave me pure joy. I couldn't wait every week to combine music, object lessons, and practical tools to expose women to their individual journeys of entering into relationship with God. When I tell you He used everything, I truly mean *everything* for my good and His glory. He wasted nothing from my process to show me His plan for me. If I had not been willing to trust Him and return to a vulnerable place, I wouldn't be writing this book today.

I hope I can encourage you to trust Him in new ways, even when you must face and wrestle with pain. Ultimately, His desire is your freedom, and He is faithful to perform every good work in you and through you. It will require you to be fearless at times, but He is big enough to handle the hard conversations. He will love you through the process, but He will ask you to lean in. It will be when you lean into Him that you begin to know His heartbeat. The heart that beats for you. No, He doesn't promise that the process will be easy, but He does promise a reward.

As we come out of the hiding places of shame to access a new perspective about fear, we step out in faith wearing the shoes of peace to Face Everything And Rise with His power pulsing on the inside, not just for our gain but for His glory. We shift our core beliefs in His ability to use each one of us, now knowing we are enough. It is in that grateful place that I am able to say, "It is well with my soul." Joy lives and abounds.

Thank you for going on this journey with me. Remember to be Fearless. It's time!

ROMANS 15:13 (NIV) *May the God of Hope fill you with all joy and peace as you trust in him, so that you may overflow with hope by the power of the Holy Spirit.*

Resources

Books

Bloom, Sandra L. *Creating Sanctuary: Toward the Evolution of Sane Societies.* Revised edition. New York: Routledge, 2013

Herman, Judith. *Trauma and Recovery.* New York: Basic Books, 2015

Jackson, Veirdre. *16 Principles for Abundant Living.* Printing Center USA, Great Falls, MT, 2017

Rosenbloom, Dena, and Mary Beth Williams. *Life after Trauma: A Workbook for Healing.* 2nd edition. New York: Guilford Press, 2010

Smedes, Lewis B. *Forgive and Forget: Healing the Hurts We Don't Deserve.* San Francisco: HarperOne, 2007

Courses

Calm Master Class on Gratitude, by Tamara Levitt, https://www.Calm.com/masterclass

Enhancing Trauma Awareness course, by Diane Wagenhals, Lakeside Global Institute, North Wales, PA https://LakesideLink.com/training

Online Articles and Resources

http://ChildTrauma.org/cta-library

"Giving Thanks Can Make You Happier," *Healthbeat,* Harvard Health Publishing, https://www.Health.Harvard.edu/healthbeat/giving-thanks-can-make-you-happier

"31 Benefits of Gratitude You Didn't Know About," Happier Human, https://www.HappierHuman.com/benefits-of-gratitude

"What Is Allostatic Load?" HRZone, https://HRZone.com/hr-glossary/what-is-allostatic-load

Wong, Joel and Joshua Brown. "How Gratitude Changes You and Your Brain," *Greater Good Magazine,* Greater Good Science Center at UC Berkeley, https://GreaterGood.Berkeley.edu/article/item/how_gratitude_changes_you_and_your_brain

Acknowledgments

AT A PIVOTAL TIME in my career, I began a process at Lakeside Global Institute (LGI) that put so many things in place for me. As an educator with decades of experience, there were things that I just knew to be true in my gut but did not have the language or depth of insight to articulate. Through my gut, I reached for children described as "hard to reach." I had a heart for them throughout my teaching career and had experienced a lot of success, but it was in my journey at LGI that I gained the scientific understanding, content knowledge, and practical tools that supported the work I had been calling my passion and opened my heart, mind, and reach beyond anything I could have dreamed of. After completing their trauma course work and eventually becoming a mentor trainer for LGI, I can honestly say it has impacted my life personally and professionally at key turning points, which has grown my desire to address adversity in not only children but in the stories of the women in their lives, which made writing this book possible. The Steps of Growth process presented for the readers of Fearless Conversations was adapted from Diane Wagenhal's copyrighted tools, teachings, and approaches at LGI and has been a game changer for me as an Iron Sharpens Iron woman reaching to help other women create actual steps of growth and change in their lives. Thank you everyone at LGI for being a part of my journey and now a part of the journey for so many others who will engage in *Fearless Conversations with a Limitless God.*

Thank you also to JNKYRD Cinema for your creativity, professionalism, and support for the project. Your commitment to each Iron Sharpens Iron Conversation allowed us to remain authentic and captured the heart of each woman's journey.

Thank you to Isaiah Pelzer for his creativity and courage to step out at 16 years old and take on the challenge of designing the artwork and coloring pages of the book. His willingness to be used by God will impact others for years to come, and I hope this experience continues to reveal the profound way God will continue to use him in his obedience to Him.

About the Author

VEIRDRE JACKSON, EdD, is a woman pursuing her purpose, passion, and life's priority to share her belief that all children deserve the best education available. She is an award-winning author, educator, and entrepreneur who is recognized as a leading educational trainer in trauma informed practices and cultural competence. She is a veteran educator with more than 20 years of experience supporting non-profit and executive leadership.

Through her experiences with systems based approaches to Trauma Awareness and Competency Development, the Resiliency Approach, and Positive Behavior and Intervention Strategies, she has harnessed her passion for building organizational resilience and strength on behalf of youth, families, and educational professionals and provides training for parents, educators, administrators, clinicians and youth development staff who desire to impact children from the inside out. Dr. Jackson is the CEO/Founder of Living Strong Consulting LLC (www.livingstrongllc.com) and the Co-Founder of Fresh Fountain of Life Counseling and Wellness. The center uses a non-traditional method of small group studies and healing through creative expression and dance. Its focus on mind, body, and spiritual health encourages women impacted by adverse experiences to live an abundant life.

She is a highly sought-after keynote speaker and consultant, working with organizations like Lakeside Global Institute as a mentor trainer, Penn State Extension as an online module developer, Pennsylvania Early Head Start as a classroom and home visiting coach, Zero to Three as a Certified trainer in Infant Toddler Competencies and the Growing Brain, and various K-12 public and chart school districts as a Cultural Competence and Relational Coach. Her book—*16 Principles for Abundant Living*—is a widely-used foundational guide for women's empowerment.

Dr. Jackson has been recognized for her expertise in professional development by Keystone Stars' Southeast Regional Key as a Professional Development Champion, is a featured presenter for the newly released 4 Part Trauma and Child Development Series by Better Kid Care, has been a contributor to *Women's Entrepreneur Magazine*, and was recognized by the *Philadelphia Business Journal* as one of 40 Leaders Under 40.

Dr. Jackson holds a Bachelor's degree from Drexel University, a Master's degree in Elementary Education from Temple University, and a Doctoral Degree from Wilmington University in Educational Leadership and Innovation. She is a wife, mother of two girls, and GiGi to her first grandson, Max.